THE COUNSELOR AND SUICIDAL CRISIS

The death of a single man is more profane
than all the words ever spoken.

— Anonymous

THE COUNSELOR AND SUICIDAL CRISIS

Diagnosis and Intervention

By

JOHN HIPPLE, Ph.D.

Psychologist, Counseling and Testing
Associate Professor, Counselor Education
North Texas State University
Denton, Texas

and

PETER CIMBOLIC, Ph.D.

Director, Counseling and Testing
Associate Professor, Psychology
North Texas State University
Denton, Texas

CHARLES C THOMAS • PUBLISHER
Springfield · Illinois · U.S.A.

Published and Distributed Throughout the World by

CHARLES C THOMAS ● PUBLISHER

Bannerstone House

301-327 East Lawrence Avenue, Springfield, Illinois, U.S.A.

© *1979, by* CHARLES C THOMAS ● PUBLISHER

ISBN 0-398-03872-4

Library of Congress Catalog Card Number: 78-21628

With THOMAS BOOKS *careful attention is given to all details of
manufacturing and design. It is the Publisher's desire to present books that
are satisfactory as to their physical qualities and artistic possibilities and
appropriate for their particular use.* THOMAS BOOKS *will be true to those
laws of quality that assure a good name and good will.*

Printed in the United States of America
V-R-1

Library of Congress Cataloging in Publication Data

Hipple, John.
   The counselor and suicidal crisis.

   Includes index.
   1. Suicide--Prevention. 2. Counseling.
   I. Cimbolic, Peter, joint author. II. Title.
   [DNLM: 1. Counseling. 2. Crisis intervention.
   3. Suicide--Prevention and control. WM401 H667c]
   RC569.H56   616.8′5844   78-21628
   ISBN 0-398-03872-4

to our families, without whose
love and support this undertaking
would not have been possible.

PREFACE

As practicing psychologists and educators, we have been aware for a number of years that there is no single, comprehensive source available to assist the practitioner in treating suicidal clients. There is a great deal of research and theory in the science of suicidology. Unfortunately, there is little that bridges the gap from the science of suicidology to the treatment of the suicidal individual. This text represents our efforts to bridge this gap.

Although the text is written for the "counselor," this term is used generically. The text is designed to assist any mental health practitioner in dealing with suicidal clients. We therefore feel this text may be helpful to the counselor, the social worker, the psychologist, the psychiatric nurse, and the pastoral counselor.

The intent of the text is to provide the counseling practitioner with a basic guide to identifying and treating the suicidal client. There is not a great deal of attention spent in identifying the theories or research in suicidology. Instead, it is a practical approach to the session-by-session struggle that the counselor and the suicidal client encounter.

From a philosophical position, it is our belief that, although an individual may have the right to take his life, we as counselors do not have the right to support this belief in the counseling process. It is our contention that the counselor must do everything in his power to prevent the death of his client. This book is predicated upon this premise.

John Hipple, Ph.D.
Peter Cimbolic, Ph.D.

Denton, Texas

ACKNOWLEDGMENTS

OUR most profound teachers have been our clients. To them is owed a special debt of gratitude. Colleagues have also given us their wisdom and knowledge. Although it is impossible to adequately recognize all of our colleagues who have given us so much, we would like to thank the following: Gerhard Nothmann, Eugene Taylor, Saul Spiro, Mary and Robert Goulding, George Thompson, and William Collins.

We also appreciate the technical assistance provided by Joseph Nagel who did so much of the leg work for the authors in our research efforts. Special thanks is also due Linda Ethridge, who so patiently typed and retyped the many drafts of this manuscript.

J. H.
P. C.

CONTENTS

	Page
Preface	vii
Acknowledgments	ix

Chapter

1. AN OVERVIEW OF SUICIDE 3

The historical, philosophical, and religious perspectives of suicide are examined. There are certain factors such as age, sex, race, and economic status which have been shown to be predictive of, or correlated with, suicide for particular groups of people. These and other considerations are discussed in relation to theories of suicide and ways in which the statistics of suicide may be interpreted.

2. DEPRESSION 15

While depression is not the exclusive emotional factor in suicidal behavior, it is very important. Particular attention must be placed on diagnosing the various depressive dimensions such as agitated vs. retarded, neurotic vs. psychotic, exogenous vs. endogenous, and primary vs. secondary depression. There are specific risk factors associated with each of these categories.

3. DIAGNOSIS OF THE SELF-DESTRUCTIVE PERSONALITY 30

Assessing the lethality level of life-threatening behavior is essential to the successful treatment of suicidal clients. Counselors must be able to differentiate between suicidal gestures and attempts, identify the stages of crisis, and be able to estimate the duration of

Chapter *Page*

the life-threatening period.

4. COUNSELING WITH THE SUICIDAL CLIENT 41

   Methods of intervening in the suicidal process are
   many and varied. The counselor must be prepared to
   be powerful and supportive as well as confrontive and
   directive. Intervention methods must change as the
   client changes, and specific techniques may be used
   only under certain conditions.

5. CONTRACTS TO STAY ALIVE AND GET WELL 65

   Having the client stay alive is the goal during all
   stages of treatment. The mechanics of negotiating
   this is a very critical task in the counseling process.
   There are many options available at this point, and
   the counselor and client must seek out the most constructive.

6. THE LIFE LINE 74

   Counseling with the suicidal client is not necessarily
   a solitary task; frequently there are significant others
   who can be helpful. It is critical for the survival of the
   client to identify and enlist the services of those
   people.

7. THE THERAPIST'S PERSONAL REACTION TO SUICIDE 82

   The counselor experiences a myriad of feelings with
   respect to his client's suicidal desires. Often these feelings facilitate the counselor's effectiveness, but perhaps as often they are debilitating to the process. The
   range of counselor feelings may include frustration,
   anger, powerlessness. It is important for the counselor
   to openly discuss these feelings with professional
   peers so that he may have the insight to continue to
   be an effective helper.

8. THE USE OF THE TELEPHONE IN TREATMENT 86

   The telephone offers the counselor a means to extend
   his availability. In using the telephone as a way to
   intervene in the suicidal crisis, the counselor must be

prepared to relate to clients in new ways. The nuances of voice quality become especially important, and the counselor must listen with acuity. Very direct questioning is frequently required in order to gain critical information.

9. LEGAL AND ETHICAL CONSIDERATIONS FOR THE

SUICIDAL CRISIS 94
There are many ethical, professional, and legal ramifications to be considered during the treatment of the suicidal client. Confidentiality is an issue that each counselor must consider as the struggle for survival develops. In some instances protection of the client involves involuntary hospitalization and the protection of life supercedes confidentiality.

10. MEDICAL AND CHEMOTHERAPEUTIC INTERVENTIONS......... 101
The benefits derived from hospitalization and the use of medicine can be very important in sustaining the life of the suicidal client. For some clients medical intervention offers a magical sense of hope; for others it is the forecast of doom. It is in the medical setting where the team approach to treatment becomes very important.

Author Index 115
Subject Index 117

THE COUNSELOR AND
SUICIDAL CRISIS

Chapter 1

AN OVERVIEW OF SUICIDE

FOR most individuals, death by any means is a disconcerting event. Death of a family member, friend, or acquaintance is usually a time of sadness, confusion, loss, grief, and even anger. Death is not always logical; to lose a loved one is an event that is difficult to comprehend. Death by means of suicide is even more difficult to understand. For most people, it is hard to empathize with someone who sees death as a method of adjustment. Most of us have only a limited understanding of why someone would choose to kill themselves.

Death is the subject of this book; in particular, death by one's own hand. It is the intent of the authors to examine the subject of suicide from the perspective of the helper. How can we as counselors intervene in the life of an individual who, for whatever reason, selected death as a means to deal with life's misfortunes? It is our contention that very few people have thought through the idea of self-destruction so that they are in a position to take their own lives based on logical and rational decision. We believe that most people who consider suicide need the assistance of a counselor so that they might avoid this irrevocable decision. We believe that suicidal thoughts, threats, and actions are most often cries for help. This book is designed to assist you, as counselors, to be better prepared to respond to that cry for help.

SUICIDE: A DEFINITION

For self-destruction to be classified as suicide, the victim must have clearly intended to kill himself; the tissue damage must have been self-inflicted; and the act must be successful. There must be no indication that the act was accidental. It is this aspect that keeps reported suicide statistics at a low level.

There are many deaths where the possibility of accident exists; consequently, the death is usually ruled as not a suicide.

Suicide as an option has been with us since life began. It appears to be a universal occurrance; while it is rare in certain cultures, it occurs everywhere. Attitudes toward suicide have varied from era to era and country to country. The so-called right of a person to kill himself has been a subject of much discussion. In early times suicide was more acceptable, but gradually it has become more and more taboo. Some countries and states have gone as far as to make self-destruction an illegal act and has been labeled self-murder or self-homicide.

STATISTICS OF SUICIDE

The suicide rate has remained relatively stable for a number of years; it usually stands at 10 or 12 deaths per 100,000 people and accounts for 1 percent of all causes of death (Frederick, 1971). As a cause of death, suicide is moving up in rank order; in 1920 it was twenty-second on the list of causes of death; in 1961 it was eleventh, and in 1976 it was ninth. In 1976, 26,800 people took their own lives while 19,500 were victims of murder.

The numbers of individuals involved in suicide attempts are enormous. An attempted suicide occurs once each minute. Approximately nine attempts take place for every one actual suicide.

Thoughts of suicide are even more common. Meerloo (1962) believes that 80 percent of all individuals will admit to having toyed with suicidal ideas.

Statistics regarding suicide are far from accurate. Because of the social stigma surrounding self-destruction, many suicides are reported as accidental deaths. It is very difficult to prove intent when the causes of death are evaluated. Because of these problems, the statistics are probably providing an underestimate of the extent of suicide; more than likely suicide occurs at a much higher rate.

CHARACTERISTICS OF THE SUICIDAL INDIVIDUAL

In general the frequency of suicide increases with age. For young people from age five to fifteen, the rate is very low, about 0.2 per 100,000. For the group of fifteen- to nineteen-year olds, the rate is 5.5 for boys and 2.0 for girls. Suicide is the fourth most frequent cause of death for individuals in this category. The rate for young people in the age range of fifteen to twenty-four has increased more than two and one-half times since the 1950s. It has increased from 4.0 in 1956 to 10.9 in 1974. For college students, suicide is second only to accidents as the leading cause of death. The suicide rates reported for this group vary from 10 to 30 per 100,000. Further, among this group the rate will vary from college to college and from grade level to grade level. The liberal arts college probably has a higher rate than the technical school, and graduate students have a higher suicide rate than undergraduates.

During the middle years, the rate climbs slightly higher. For the elderly the rate of suicide attempts recedes, but the rate of completed attempts is the highest of all groups. Generally speaking, the age is lower for those who attempt as compared to those who complete suicide. Consequently, states which have the highest number of elderly people have higher suicide rates.

Geographical differences are also apparent when examining suicide rates. Nevada frequently will have the highest rate among all states. San Francisco will often have the highest rate among cities. Cities in the South generally have lower suicide rates. In general, urban suicides exceed rural suicides.

According to sex, women attempt suicide at a rate three times higher than men. Women homemakers make twice as many suicide attempts as women in all work classifications. However, men actually kill themselves at a higher rate than women and account for approximately 70 percent of the deaths. Men usually employ more violent or more lethal means of self-destruction such as guns or by hanging, while women will use poison, pills, or gas. The less lethal means used by women increase the chance of being rescued, thereby explaining the lower rate of suicide completion.

In recent years, however, the differences between men and women have been changing. Women are currently using more lethal means of self-destruction; consequently, more are succeeding at their attempts. The rates for young professional women are very close to the rate for similar groups of men.

Married people, except for the very young married, kill themselves at a lower rate than the single individual. Widows under age thirty-five have a higher rate than older widows. Having children to care for usually reduces the rate. Those who have been widowed or divorced kill themselves more often than those who have never been married.

Along religious lines, Protestants have a higher suicide rate than Catholics or Jews; however, most research has not examined the area of religiousity. It is not known if there is a difference between those who attend church frequently as opposed to those who do not.

With respect to socioeconomic status, the highest and the lowest groups kill themselves at the greater rates. In the middle class, the rate peaks among members of certain professions, usually doctors, lawyers, and dentists. Some statistics show an increase as one goes up the economic scale; Maris (1969) found in Chicago that the middle class as a whole had the lowest rates.

Further, rates of suicide will vary as to the social and political pressures of the times. During depressions rates will increase in all economic classes. During times of war the rates will generally decrease.

Racial origin of the individual will also be a factor in suicidal rate. In the South, whites kill themselves twice as frequently as blacks. In the North, the rate for young black males is twice as high as young whites. For those over age thirty-five, the rate for blacks levels out while the rate for whites goes up. The young American Indian has a rate much higher than the young black.

The time of the year has also been shown to impact suicide rates. Spring is the time of the year when the suicide rate is the highest. April is often the highest single month. Christmas is one holiday season when the rate will be slightly higher.

When a psychological autopsy is carried out on the suicidal victim, it is usually found that the person has been suffering from a rather clear case of neurosis, alcoholism, or some other psychological disorder. Approximately 5 percent of all suicide victims have been suffering from physical illness. In only about 5 percent of all suicides can no preexisting emotional or physical illness be found.

Approximately 80 percent of those who kill themselves have communicated their intent in one way or another. The message can be extremely subtle, however. About 12 percent of those who attempt suicide will make another attempt and succeed within a two-year time span. For those who do kill themselves, four out of five have attempted at least once before.

RELIGIOUS AND PHILOSOPHICAL POINTS OF VIEW

The moral views of suicide vary from era to era and society to society. For the most part, suicide has not been seen as an acceptable means of dealing with one's reality. On religious grounds, suicide is a crime against God; generally, with some exception, the act can be forgiven. For those of the Jewish faith, suicide is a breach of one of the Ten Commandments, but it can be forgiven since it is assumed that the act is carried out by the emotionally disturbed. For many Christians, the tenets of the church are more strict, and suicide is looked upon with extreme disfavor. Taking of life is not to be accomplished by man's own hand. Because of the sinfulness of suicide, some churches will not bury the victim in hallowed ground. Moslems, also, are forbidden to commit suicide. Buddhists and Hindus, however, are more tolerant of self-destruction. There is also the ritualistic suicide that is not uncommon among Japanese when the situation involves an issue of honor. Another example, in this vein, is the accepting attitude toward the Brahman widow who has thrown herself on the funeral pyre of her husband.

Suicide has been discussed by philosophers over the ages. Some, as Camus, have been opposed to it, while others, such as Hume have taken a neutral accepting stance. Groups such as the Stoics have even seen suicide as a laudable practice. The concept of free will often enters these discussions; should man, as an individual, be allowed the ultimate freedom of deciding if life is worth living. There is certainly no agreement as to the answer.

Situational ethics are sometimes used in judging the rightness or wrongness of suicide. The physically healthy individual who considers suicide may be much differently viewed than the terminally ill or aged person who also considers self-destruction. For the individual who is obviously emotionally ill, forgiveness for the suicidal act is more likely to occur. The value placed on stress varies from person to person; in the lives of most people, at one time or another, there well may be a reason to commit suicide. Because of these factors, it has been very difficult for philosophers and religious thinkers to come to agreement on the ethical and moral issue of suicide.

LEGAL VIEWS OF SUICIDE

Frederick (1971) discusses the taboo which encompasses the subject of suicide. For most individuals, suicide is a totally unacceptable behavior. Consequently, there are many direct and indirect sanctions that come into play when an individual threatens, attempts, or commits suicide. These sanctions have a long-standing base in history with many originating in Roman, Church, and English law. The law most often states that an individual does not have the right to kill himself. Most often the sanctions were placed on the property of the deceased, with the state receiving some portion of the estate of the person who has killed himself. Currently, a few states still have laws on the books which make suicide a crime. These laws are very seldom enforced against those who attempt suicide but fail to complete the act. Most insurance companies will not honor a life insurance policy for an individual who kills himself.

PSYCHOLOGICAL AND SOCIOLOGICAL VIEWS

Psychologically, there have been many theories developed

which have examined the suicidal personality. It is interesting to note that it was not until the nineteenth century that suicide came to be considered a psychological problem. Freud discussed the issue of the life instinct versus the drive toward death or destruction. Adler talked about the inferior feelings which are inherent in all individuals. Sullivan viewed suicide as the struggle between the good me, bad me, and not me. Horney discussed suicide in relation to the interaction between the individual and the environment. Menninger believes that suicide is based on inner feelings of hate, guilt, and hopelessness. For the most part, psychological theories put the emphasis on understanding the individual's perspective; therefore, suicidal ideation must be studied in light of the internal emotional make-up.

Social theorists believe that, if a complete picture of suicide is to be developed, such factors as the individual's role and status in his social system must be examined and understood. Man does not stand alone; his relevance is most often based on his relationship to that which is around him. Consequently, the understanding of suicide is best achieved by looking at both personal and social systems.

Durkheim's work in the late nineteenth century was one of the first comprehensive efforts to examine suicide. He believed that suicide varies inversely with the degree of integration of the suicider's social group. A social group is integrated to the extent that the members share beliefs and sentiments and are interested in each other. Rate is also influenced by the extent of social control; groups with either high or low social control were predicted to have the higher rates. Durkheim went on to identify four types of suicides: egoistic, referring to the person not integrated in any group; the altruistic suicide refers to the person who feels it is his duty to kill himself (an example would be the warrior who looses face); anomic suicide occurs when there are no norms or rules, or when there is a loss of orientation (widowhood could be an example); and fatalistic suicide happens when there is too much regulation and control (the suicide of a slave would be an illustration). There are many examples of mixed types of suicide; it can be very difficult to clearly place an individual into one of these categories.

QUALITY OF THE RESEARCH

To say the least, research in the area of suicide is fragmentary. Many studies do not build on other investigations, so results are difficult to integrate. Research is difficult to pursue in this area. The individual who commits suicide is not around to participate in any investigation. It is very difficult to do comparisons using control groups because of the vagueness of criteria for assigning people to groups of high or low suicidal risk. Ethical and professional issues also make research more difficult. For example, if one believes that the suicidal individuals deserve the best possible treatment, then a potentially suicidal person cannot be assigned to a no-treatment control group. Examination of demographic patterns is difficult to accomplish because of different reporting systems and criteria for establishing whether or not an act was of a suicidal nature.

Data may be interpreted in many ways. There is certainly much common sense that can be applied to interpreting different patterns of suicide rate. For example, one might hypothesize that it is the pressure of the profession that sets the stage for the high rate for physicians or that it is the despondency of living without hope that is involved in the high rate among American Indians. However, we must acknowledge that these are assumptions and not facts; unfortunately, these interpretations of data are often treated as if they were fact.

We also know that numerical difference is not the same as a statistically significant difference in the rates between two groups. Yet, it is not uncommon for nonsignificant differences to be treated as if they were significant just because a difference was found. This is exemplified by the interpretation of differential rates occurring during holidays. Christmas may be a high point, but from a statistical viewpoint the rate between it and other holidays is not significantly different. Further, because of the lack of discriminating data, we cannot actually say there are differences as to day of the week or time of day with respect to suicide rate.

It is not unusual for one investigation to conclude one thing and another investigation to conclude something else, or for rates found to occur in one geographic location to be generalized to the whole nation. All of these examples of inappropriate research conclusions suggest cautious consumption. Readers need to be aware that research must be examined with care; the state of the research art is such that reasons for differences are not yet firmly established, and further, differences that are reported may not represent "real" differences.

To improve our data collection and the conclusions derived from that process, the scientific method must continue to be applied to the field with increasing rigor. Definitions of terms must be established, systems of reporting information improved, continued attempts to establish control groups must be made, and statistical treatment must be improved — these are but a few of the steps that are required.

Theory building and testing of these theories must continue. Presently, there is little integration of the available data on suicide with the existing theories of suicidal behavior or of suicide data and theory with more general theories of behavior. In addition, continuity in research, as it is applied to one investigation being built from previous studies, is equally important and up until now has not been done. Continued efforts to integrate this checkerboard picture of research will go a long way in improving our understanding of suicidal behavior.

CURRENT CLASSIFICATIONS OF SUICIDE

In order for adequate research and theory building to proceed, standard classification systems of suicidal behavior are required.

Classifications in this area are very difficult to construct because of the many differences in approaches and variability in the data base. It is not easy to formulate a general construct which will hold up across the many human variables which are involved in suicide. A beginning place is to categorize different types of suicidal behavior. Lester (1972) has outlined the following: completed suicide, attempted suicide, threats of suicide, thoughts of suicide, and no preoccupation with suicide. Shneidman (1963) looked at suicide from the view that it is just another form of death and developed the following classification: (1) The intended suicide is a person who makes every attempt to guarantee that his self-destructive act will be successful. (2) Subintention people pursue death in a less certain and often indirect fashion; the chronic substance abuser is an example. (3) Unintentional individuals fall into the accidental or natural death category as they play no part in their own death. (4) Contraintended people are those who feign suicide by drinking water out of a washed-out iodine bottle, or the person who threatened suicide but has no intention of taking real action.

Neuringer (1974) has compiled an extensive classification list: (1) Intentional suicide involves the individual engaging in self-destruction with full awareness of the consequences. (2) Psychotic suicide refers to any act which may not have death as the ultimate end; a cutting out of the bad parts of the body is an example. (3) Automatization suicide is typified by the person who takes one barbituate pill after another with no conscious thought of the possible result. (4) Chronic suicide describes the individual who is being self-destructive in a long-term manner such as the substance abuser. (5) Manipulation suicide describes any attempt of low lethality usually with the intent serving as a warning or a plea for help. An example might be an individual cutting his wrist in the presence of others. (6) Accidental suicide pictures the individual whose attempt backfired and death was the result; the person who wanted to be rescued but whose spouse came home later than usual and could not save their life. These people miscalculate their rescue plans. (7) Neglect suicide describes the person who dies because he neglected to provide proper health care, as the coronary patient who ignores the physician's advice and dies through overwork. (8) Probability suicide refers to those who gamble with their lives such as the race car driver or the person who plays Russian Roulette. (9) Self-destructive suicide describes the overeater or the heavy smoker or the person who frequently runs stop lights. (10) Suicidal threats are those who only talk but have no intention of action. (11) Suicidal thinking is quite frequent but does not involve talk or action. (12) Test suicide refers to the individual whose responses on a test such as the MMPI or one of the projectives indicates suicidal tendencies.

Classifications are but the first step in developing an understanding of suicide. As we can come to agreement regarding definitions, we will be in a better position to develop theories and gather and analyze the available data.

A PERSONAL THEORY

Every counselor must have in mind a general theory or at least a philosophical stance regarding suicide. This can vary from believing that suicide is an act of free will, which should not be interfered with, to believing that any suicidal act or threat is a cry for help and requires active intervention. Once the basic belief is formulated, then each counselor can go on to develop a personal style of counseling with the suicidal client.

SUMMARY

It is easily seen that there are many points from which to view suicide. Factors such as definition, historical perspective, religious and philosophical stances, statistical interpretations, sociological foundations, and the individual's psychological base are some of the major points to consider. Even among suicidal individuals there is a great deal of difference. The person who takes a pistol and places it in his mouth and pulls the trigger is very different from the person who uses a razor blade to make slight cuts on his wrist. The basic intent and the resultant dangerousness of the act is different. As the suicides are different, so are approaches to counseling with them. The approach taken in working with a suicidal client varies from client to client and from professional to professional. It is the intent of this book to open the door for the reader. How the reader assimilates this material and uses it will be an individual matter.

REFERENCES

Frederick, Calvin J.: The present suicide taboo in the United States. *Ment Hyg, 55*:178-183, 1971.

Lester, David: *Why People Kill Themselves.* Springfield, Thomas, 1972.

Maris, Ronald W.: *Social Forces in Urban Suicide.* Homewood, Dorsey, 1969.

Meerloo, Joost A.M.: *Suicide and Mass Suicide.* New York, Grune, 1962.

Neuringer, Charles: *Psychological Assessment of Suicidal Risk.* Springfield, Thomas, 1974.

Shneidman, Edwin S.: Orientations toward death. *The Study of Lives: Essays on Personality in Honor of Henry A. Murray.* New York, Atherton, 1963.

SUGGESTED READINGS

Durkheim, Emile: *Suicide.* Translated by J. A. Spaulding and George Simpson. New York, Free Pr, 1951, (original, 1897).

Ellis, Edward R. and Allen, George N.: *Traitor Within: Our Suicide Problem.* Garden City, Doubleday, 1961.

Farberow, Norman L.: *Suicide in Different Cultures.* Baltimore, Univ Park, 1975.

Farberow, Norman L. and Shneidman, Edwin S.: *The Cry for Help.* New York, McGraw, 1961.

Gibbs, Jack P.: *Suicide.* New York, Har-Row, 1968.

Hillman, James: *Suicide and the Soul.* New York, Har-Row, 1964.

Klagsbrun, Francine: *Too Young to Die, Youth and Suicide.* Boston, HM, 1976.

Kobler, Arthur L. and Stotland, Ezra: *The End of Hope: A Social-Clinical Study of Suicide.* New York, Free Pr, 1964.

Lester, Gene and Lester, David: *Suicide the Gamble with Death.* Englewood Cliffs, P-H, 1971.

Resnik, H. L. P.: *Teaching Outlines in Suicide Studies and Crisis Intervention.* Bowie, Md, Charles, 1974.

Shneidman, Edwin S. (Ed.): *Essays in Self-destruction.* New York, Science House, 1967.

Shneidman, Edwin S.: *Suicidology: Contemporary Developments.* New York, Grune, 1976.

Shneidman, Edwin S., Farberow, Normal L., and Litman, Robert E. (Eds.): *The Psychology of Suicide.* New York, Science House, 1970.

Waldenstrom, Jan, Larsson, Tage, and Ljungstedt, Nils (Eds.): *Suicide and Attempted Suicide.* Stockholm, Nordiska Bokhandelns Forlag, 1972.

Wolman, Benjamin B. and Krauss, Herbert H.: *Between Survival and Suicide.* New York, Gardner, 1976.

Chapter 2

DEPRESSION

In each counselor's training he has probably been taught to be sensitive to suicide potential in people who are depressed. The role of depression in suicide causality has long been recognized. What has been unclear is differentiation of the various types of depression and the ensuing suicidal risk as a function of each type of depression.

In examining depression it is often helpful to consider it on a series of dichotomous dimensions. However, in actuality, these dimensions are probably not dichotomous but rather are continuous variables with the extremes being towards either end of the dichotomy.

The most commonly recognized depressive dichotomies include the following: agitated-retarded, neurotic-psychotic, exogenous-endogenous, and primary-secondary depressions. It is our contention that most depressions are not purely one or the other on any of these dichotomies, but rather, probably "load" towards one end or the other of the various continuums. Further, it is probably in the clinician's best interest to consider each of these continuums in the evaluation of the depressed client. Once the client is evaluated along each of these continuums, the "loadings" on each of these dimensions should be integrated into one statement that would best describe the existing depression. For example, a patient may be best described as exhibiting an agitated-neurotic-exogenous-primary depression. By so combining and integrating these continuums into one diagnostic statement about the depression, the clinician is in a better position to assess the suicidal risk, in that the risk factors associated with each of the loadings on each of the continuums are probably close to additive in function in the assessment of suicidal risk.

AGITATED VERSUS RETARDED DEPRESSION

Agitated depression is characterized by directionless activity, often debilitating anxiety, frequent crying episodes, feelings of losing control, and despair. One characteristic that is blatantly apparent in these patients is their overwhelming psychic anguish. These patients present a great suicidal risk in that they are in obvious immediate psychic pain and have a great deal of undirected energies. There is an immediacy about these patients in that they want the pain to be over now. It is this urgency which presents the greatest suicidal danger. These patients are both depressed and have the energy to do something about it. The agitated, depressed client is not likely to have well-thought-through suicidal plans but nonetheless is at great risk in that he will be driven to the impulsive attempt to end his torment. Therefore, the suicidal risk is extremely great while the patient is in the throes of the agitated depression. Fortunately, this type of depression is more likely to resolve itself quickly.

Retarded depression is more likely to have an insidious onset and is most often of longer duration than agitated depression. Retarded depression is characterized by extreme apathy to others and the environment. The client is usually not anxious nor agitated. Although the client is significantly depressed, the client does not fight the depression. It is as if the client has resigned himself to the depression and has given up. Consequently, the suicidal risk is less acute at any given moment when compared to the agitated depression, but the client experiencing retarded depression may be as likely to kill himself over time in that he remains depressed for a longer duration. As suggested by Shneidman et. al. (1970), a further danger with the retarded depression is that, as the depression starts to resolve itself and the client seems to be experiencing an improvement in his behavior pattern, the therapist as well as his "others" relax, since they are deluded into thinking that he is cured. It is at this time that the person has the intensity and strength to actually go through with his suicide attempt.

According to Shneidman et. al. (1970), most suicides as a

function of depression take place in a fairly short amount of time, ranging from a few days to three months, after the client has seemingly begun to improve. They also suggest that any significant behavioral change, even if it appears to be a positive one, should be considered as a possible index of suicide. In light of this, it is critical that the client's significant others be informed of the "course" that this type of depression is likely to follow. Particularly, it is important that they be aware of the increased suicidal risk as retarded depression is resolving.

In summation, the agitated depression represents the more acute suicidal risk. The retarded depressive, although not as acutely suicidal, may be as great a suicidal risk in that he is usually depressed for longer periods of time. Also, the retarded depressive may become more actively suicidal as the depression starts to lift. When this occurs, the depression is less retarded and the client has greater psychic energy with which to become acutely suicidal.

NEUROTIC VERSUS PSYCHOTIC DEPRESSION

Neurosis is most typically defined as unresolved internalized conflict, with the predominant feature being anxiety. In neurotic depression the above is true but with depression either being the presenting complaint or it being obviously evident. The client has not lost contact with reality as in psychotic depression. His functioning is impaired but not to such a degree that he is totally ineffective in dealing with reality as seen in psychotic depression. The neurotic depressive typically experiences frequent crying episodes over which he feels he has no control. This makes the client increasingly anxious, in turn making him further depressed and increasing the likelihood of another crying episode. This is a terribly painful cycle.

Clients experiencing neurotic depression are also likely to be very "public" with their depression. Family, friends, and doctors are all likely to be the target of the client's constant "help" seeking. The family often "tires" of this constant support-seeking behavior. Therefore, suicidal behavior is likely to result in order that the client can impress upon others how serious his problems are.

Neurotic depression is most often precipitated by external events. It is the "over-reaction" to these events that defines the reaction as neurotic, and the depression lasts far longer than one would expect in considering the precipitant. As Paykel (1976) reports, "Life events, particularly exit events and events regarded as undesirable, cluster prior to the onset of depression." Again, it is the degree of the reaction and the duration that one considers in making the determination as to whether it is indeed neurotic. There is a serious suicidal risk associated with neurotic depression. Pokorney (1964) reports 119 suicide cases per 100,000 per year for neurotic depressions as compared with the United States national rate of about 10 per 100,000 per year for the general population. Further, Miles (1977) reports that 15 percent of neurotic depressives die by suicide. From Helgason's data (1964) 2.5 percent of the population will at some time suffer from neurotic depression, and he also suggests that as many as 15 percent of depressive neurotics die by suicide. Thompson and Hendrie (1972) state, "It is especially to be noted that the diagnosis of neurotic or reactive depression confers at least as high a risk of suicide as does the diagnosis of endogenous depression."

Psychotic depression is, of course, a more debilitating depression. To arrive at this diagnosis, one must first establish the presence of a psychosis. The most common diagnostic benchmarks in establishing this diagnosis include the inability to engage in reality testing, the inability to function in reality, serious decompensation of ego functioning, impoverished interpersonal relationships, and lack of insight into their pathology. When depression affects the client to the point that any or all of the above are true, the client is probably experiencing a depression of psychotic magnitude.

Psychotic depressions are of two types, unipolar and bipolar. Unipolar depressions are those in which the depression is "autonomous" in that it is a "pure" depressive disorder. In unipolar depression there is no history of manic cycles. Most often these depressions are considered to be endogenous in that there is usually accompanying vegetative and metabolic signs, e.g.

loss of appetite, weight loss, insomnia, etc. Bassuk and Schoonover (1977) contend that only about 15 percent of clinical depressions fall into this category. It is important to keep in mind that unipolar psychotic depressions are not necessarily endogenous in nature, although they typically are. As to whether unipolar depressions are endogenous may seem academic, but it becomes important in the evaluation for possible medication interventions.

Unipolar depressions, as are most of the major affective disorders, are cyclical in nature, i.e. once a patient has a history of unipolar depression, it is extremely likely that he will experience episodes in the future. Most often the depression-free periods are from three to five years, but of course there is a great deal of variability in the length of time of these cycles. It is during these depressive episodes that the clients are most likely to become suicidal. Since these depressions are psychotic, these clients most often are hospitalized. It is ironic that the greatest suicidal risk occurs *after* the patient is discharged from the hospital. It has been our experience that a suicidal crisis is most typically six weeks in length. Most hospitalizations for serious depressive illness are two to three weeks. It takes approximately two to three weeks for antidepressant medication to be effective. Once the depression starts to lift the patient is likely to be discharged from the hospital. Therefore, when the patient leaves the hospital he is less depressed, not psychotic, but he now has the psychic energy with which to kill himself. Most suicides of those people who have been hospitalized for depression is within a month of their discharge from the hospital. Therefore, it is imperative that the patient, upon discharge, continue to be in counseling and be closely monitored.

Hospitalization presents problems for the nonmedical therapist. The client is typically in treatment with a counselor who recognizes the need for the client to be hospitalized. The counselor then typically makes the hospitalization arrangements and/or refers the client to a psychiatrist. It is here that the communication often breaks down. The counselor *assumes* the psychiatrist will take complete responsibility for the client. This assumption is warranted while the patient is in the hospital but may not be valid once the patient is discharged. It is imperative that the counselor and the psychiatrist make an explicit agreement, while the patient is in the hospital, as to who will be responsible for follow-up care upon the patient's discharge. Very often the patient will be under the psychiatrist's care for the monitoring of medications, but the psychiatrist would prefer that the patient remain in therapy with the original counselor, particularly if the counselor had a well-established relationship with the client prior to the hospitalization. It is important to keep in mind, however, the ultimate disposition of the client rests with the psychiatrist; it is he who has the responsibility to decide whether to refer back to the original counselor. We must reiterate the importance of posthospitalization treatment responsibility being resolved before the patient's discharge from the hospital. It has been our experience, when this is not done, too many clients slip through the communication gap that we have in part created, with the tragedy of continued suicide risk.

Bipolar depression is considered in the context of a manic-depressive disorder. To establish the diagnosis of bipolar depression, there has to have been both a depressive and a manic episode of psychotic proportion. The DSM-III draft, *Diagnostic and Statistical Manual of Mental Disorders*, prepared by The Task Force on Nomenclature and Statistics of The American Psychiatric Association (1978), indicates that Bipolar Affective Disorders are most likely to manifest in the form of a manic episode typically before the age of thirty. They further state, "Both the Manic and The Depressive Episodes are more frequent and shorter than in either Manic or Major Depressive Disorder. Frequently a Manic or Depressive Episode will be followed immediately by a short period of the other kind. In rare cases, over long periods of time there is an alternation of the two kinds of episodes without a normal interval period (cycling)." The interim symptom-free periods may be months or years of normal functioning.

With respect to suicidal risk, the transition phase of a psychotic episode in which the patient is either moving from a manic episode into a depression, or when the patient is moving from a depressive state to a manic one, is particularly dangerous. This is not to say that there is no suicidal risk in the purely depressed state or the purely manic one. In the manic state, suicidal ideation is usually not apparent since the primary defensive structure is predicated around the client's denial that anything is wrong. However, it is this massive denial that is often dynamically interpreted as extreme compensatory behavior designed to protect the client from having to deal with the overwhelming underlying depression. Therefore, these clients are more apt to take extreme risks behaviorally because of their delusional feelings of invincibility. In fact behaviors are probably unconscious suicidal attempts or gestures. Again, these patients are likely to be treated in a hospital setting but prior to the hospitalization will often be in counseling with a nonmedical therapist. It is important for the counselor to recognize the early signs of the manic episode so the patient can be referred for in-patient psychiatric care as early as possible. It is equally important for the counselor to exercise, or attempt to exercise, some control over the manic client's behavior prior to hospitalization. This can best be done by sharing with the significant others of the client and alerting them to the potential "accidental" suicide attempt. It is our opinion that every manic client should be considered a possible suicidal risk.

With respect to the depressive phase of the bipolar disorder, the risk of suicide is in direct proportion to the degree of agitation present. The client who is extremely lethargic, depressed, noncommunicative, not crying, and has lost complete interest in his environment is less likely to kill himself since he does not have the energy to attempt or the clarity of thought to develop a plan. It is the agitated depressive with crying, hopelessness, despair, and desperation that is the more likely suicidal candidate. However, the risk increases, as previously stated, if the depression starts lifting and the client is moving towards a manic phase. Although bipolar affective disorders are less common than unipolar depressions, the DSM-III Draft (1978) indicated that from .4 to 1.2 percent of the adult population have had Bipolar Affective Disorders.

EXOGENOUS VERSUS ENDOGENOUS DEPRESSION

Exogenous depressions are those depressions in which the causes of the depression lie external to the individual. Exogenous depression is often referred to as reactive depression and is most often precipitated by the experiencing of loss by the client. This loss may be the loss of employment, of loved one, of position, or of self-esteem. Exogenous depressions may be of either neurotic or psychotic magnitude, although most often it does not reach psychotic proportion. It is in the response to this loss that the person is likely to become suicidal. The individual, in his grief over the loss or his feelings that he cannot exist without that which was lost, chooses to end his existence. It is important to assess the potential suicidal risk for any client who appears to be consistent with the description above. Most often these clients, through counseling, can come to accept that that which was lost, important as it may have been to their lives, can be lived without, and they may come to view other alternatives in themselves to replace the loss. Until this realization is reached by the client, however, the risk of suicide remains and may become extreme.

Endogenous depressions are defined as those in which the client exhibits a number of biological signs. The typical symptom picture includes: decrease in appetite, weight loss, difficulty in falling asleep, difficulty in maintaining sleep, early morning awakening without being able to fall back to sleep, inability to experience pleasure, decreased interest in sex, constipation, family history of depression, and family history of favorable response to antidepressant medication. Another symptom differentiating endogenous from exogenous depression is that in endogenous depression mood is worse in the morning and improves as day goes on, whereas in exogenous depression the client's mood is more likely to be good in the morning and becomes progressively depressed as the day goes on. Current thought explains the cause of these depressions in the context of the biogenic amine hypothesis (Bassuk & Schoonover, 1977) which suggests there is a depletion of catecholamines at central adrenegeric sites in the brain. The antidepressant medications serve to rectify this imbalance in brain chemistry.

As with exogenous depression, endogenous depression may be of either neurotic or psychotic magnitude. It should also be pointed out that an endogenous depression of neurotic proportion can evolve into a psychotic depression. If there is a chemical imbalance in the brain, this condition if untreated with medications could become worse and shift the depression from neurotic to psychotic.

Endogenous depressions are usually more persistent than exogenous depressions. Therefore, although the suicidal risk may be less at any given moment for the endogenous depressive, the cumulative risk may be greater, in that the patient will be depressed for a longer period and also is likely to have many depressive episodes.

The treatment for endogenous depressions should include the use of major antidepressant medications, most often the tricyclics. It is important to note that many times the counselor remains the primary therapist as the client uses his family physician to prescribe antidepressants. This can serve to fragment the care. It is necessary for the counselor to stay in close communication with the prescribing physician and it is important for the counselor to realize that it will take from two to six weeks for the medication to be effective in alleviating the depression. While we give antidepressants to depressed people who are suicidal, we are also giving them an excellent means to kill themselves — the antidepressants. When taken in large amounts, the antidepressants can be extremely life-threatening. The counselor should involve the family of the client who is endogenously depressed as well as suicidal. The family should be involved in the dispensing and control of the medication while the client is in this precarious condition. If the family is responsible for the dispensing of these medications, it may avoid the client attempting to overdose.

Endogenous depressions present additional problems with respect to suicidal risk. Endogenous depressions are extremely likely to recur, particularly if the client discontinues the medication prematurely. Further, if a patient was suicidal during one depressive episode, it can be expected the client will become suicidal in ensuing episodes. The diagnostic difficulty for the counselor rests in endogenous depressions, since they are unlikely to be precipitated by external events. Therefore, the counselor does not have the life-stress warning signs he is likely to have in reactive-exogenous depressions. Endogenous depressions just seem to happen.

The distinction with actual clients between endogenous and exogenous depressions is often very difficult to determine. Most depressions are neither clearly endogenous or exogenous, but rather "load" towards the exogenous or endogenous end of the continuum. It is the extent that they "load" that would determine the course of treatment, particularly with respect to medication interventions.

Another point to consider in looking at depression in the endogenous-exogenous context is the "Which came first, the chicken or the egg?" argument. Do changes in brain chemistry produce depression, or does depression produce changes in brain chemistry? In fact, both probably take place simultaneously in some cases. It is possible to have a depression clearly precipitated by an external event that persists over time and takes on more and more endogenous characteristics. The counselor should be on the alert for this phenomenon.

PRIMARY VERSUS SECONDARY DEPRESSION

Primary depressions are those in which there is no history of psychiatric illness, other than affective episodes, nor are they the secondary consequence of any other physical disease. Secondary depressions are those that are the consequence of some other primary diagnosis, i.e. depression following a heart attack, depression associated with diabetes, depression associated with childbirth, depression associated with other psychiatric illness, etc. The primary-secondary concept of depression is probably dichotomous and not on a continuum as are the two-way classifications of depression previously considered. Therefore, the diagnostic differentiation is not as problematic as with the other depressive classifications. All the other classifications of depression could be further subcategorized as either primary or secondary in nature, i.e. primary neurotic depression, secondary neurotic depression associated with childbirth, etc.

The suicidal risk associated with the primary depressions have been discussed elsewhere in this chapter.

Secondary depressions diagnostically are nebulous. Since these depressions occur in the presence of a primary disorder, it is often the primary disorder alone that gets treated without recognizing the early signs of a developing depression. An example of this follows: A young man at a major university sustained a serious knee injury during an intercollegiate football contest. This young man, previous to the injury, had only one aspiration after graduation from college — to play professional football. The orthopedic surgeon corrected the massive injuries to the knee and also told the patient that it would be unlikely he would ever play football again. His family noticed the young man became significantly depressed after the surgery, but felt it was to be expected and really did not think much of it. After he returned to campus, one of the authors was contacted by the head football coach expressing concern over recent behavioral changes exhibited by this student. The young man, who had previously been quite shy and retiring, most recently had become quite talkative and outgoing. Upon hearing the student's most recent history, it was recommended that the student be urged to seek out psychological evaluation. The student accepted the football coach's recommendation and was evaluated by a counselor. It became apparent during the interview that the patient was exhibiting massive denial and that the only reason he had consented to see a counselor was to placate his coach. Although the patient was encouraged to enter counseling, the patient did not feel it was necessary at that time. About two weeks passed when the football coach again called quite alarmed about the student. This time, the student just had a massive spending spree in which he had bought his friend a new automobile. (The student was of modest means.) The student was again brought to the university health service and further evaluated. It was apparent that the young man was in an acute manic episode. After treatment with medications and over time, the young man further developed an acute depressive episode. At this time his feelings of doom and uselessness associated around the feelings of not being ever able to play football again came to the surface. All of the time leading up to this event and subsequent to his surgery, people were most concerned about how his leg was healing; his peers in particular were continually encouraging the student that once his leg was better of course he would be able to return to the football squad. Dynamically, his peers were encouraging his denial. The point here, however, is that everyone was paying attention to the injury and no one was paying attention to the student's feelings associated around the potential consequence of the injury.

The above case is really not atypical. Although specialist physicians are increasingly paying greater attention to the psychological impact of disease and injury, we as counselors must be even more vigilant. It is too common that people pay attention to the progress of a physical problem and ignore the feelings of the patient. One could easily understand why secondary depressions are so common, as well as understand how often appropriate psychological interventions are delayed unnecessarily. Once a secondary depression does develop, it is important for the counselor to work in close coordination with the physician who had been treating the "primary" problem. By so doing, the counselor can benefit from the physician's experience with the present client as well as other similar cases the physician may have treated in the past. Further, the physician can share with the counselor whether the depression may be an actual symptom of the disease that is being treated (as in diabetes). Lastly, the physical condition of the patient may preclude the use of antidepressants which may have normally been considered in treating the depression.

With respect to the suicidal risk of any secondary depression, it is not a function of the depression as being "secondary" but rather a function of the type of depression discussed elsewhere in this chapter. Each of the depressions previously discussed may be a "secondary" depression to other illnesses. Of course, as far as the counselor is concerned with respect to his treatment, it is the depression that is of primary concern.

GENERAL COMMENTS ABOUT DEPRESSION AND OTHER MENTAL ILLNESSES OF SUICIDAL RISK

Within the depressive disorders, factors other than the severity or the kind of depression also must be considered in ascertaining suicidal risk. Lester and Beck (1975) in a study of 254 attempted suicides found that hopelessness was a better predictor of suicidal intent than other aspects of depression. They further found that negative outlook, anhedonia, and psychomotor retardation were related to suicidal intent while guilt, anorexia, and irritability did not seem to be related to suicidal risk. Shneidman et al. (1970) suggest four ominous signs of suicide potentiality in depressives: (1) an impatient, agitated attitude that something must be done immediately; (2) a detailed, feasible, lethal suicide plan; (3) pride, suspicion, and extreme independence as character traits; and (4) isolation, withdrawal, living alone, or living with someone so extremely emotionally isolated from the client that he is in effect living alone.

The content of this chapter until now has primarily concerned itself with "clinically significant depression." It is not only depressed people who kill themselves, however. Further, many people who kill themsleves would not be diagnosed as having a mental illness. Miles (1977) indicates that a great many suicides occur among those with reactive depression and that reactive depression is not strictly mental illness but is a normal reaction of any individual to sufficiently severe stress — there does not appear to be sufficient evidence to rule out this "normal reaction" hypothesis (to suicide). The above hypothesis is critical. In a great many counseling settings such as university and college counseling centers and schools, the vast majority of the clientele is not diagnosable in the traditional mental illness model. At best, the diagnosis of many of these clients would be a transient situational disturbance. This is not to rule out, however, the possibility of suicidal risk. It is important for the counselor to keep in mind the possibility of suicidal risk with any client who is experiencing a reaction to significant loss in their life.

Even in those human conditions that may be classified as mental illness, depression is not the only diagnosis in which the counselor will encounter the possibility of serious suicidal risk. Winokur and Tsuang (1975) in using thirty- to forty-year follow-up data on discharged mental patients, found for 76 manic patients, 82 depressives, and 170 schizophrenics that 10 percent of the schizophrenics, 8.5 percent of the manics, and 10.6 percent of the depressives who were deceased had died by suicide. They further suggest that suicide is more likely to occur at an earlier age in schizophrenics than in the other illnesses. Pokorney (1964) demonstrated similar findings. He found the suicide rate per 100,000 per year to be the following: depressives, 566; schizophrenics, 167; neurotics, 119; personality disorders, 130; alcoholism, 133; and organic brain syndromes, 78. These rates are all strikingly higher than the nationwide rate of 10 per 100,000.

The above data clearly reveals that mental illness per se increases the likelihood of suicide. For the counselor, perhaps the most difficult group for which to ascertain suicidal risk would be the schizophrenics. Of all the diagnostic groups considered above, schizophrenics are the second most likely group to kill themselves. Doctor Michael Peck, of the Los Angeles Suicide Prevention Center, at a recent symposium (Preventing the Youthful Suicide, 1977) indicated that the most common diagnosis in college students who had committed suicide was schizophrenia. The difficulty in ascertaining the suicidal risk with the client suffering from schizophrenia is there is less likely to be active suicidal warnings. The suicide risk with schizophrenics is further compounded by their lack of reality testing. The schizophrenic is very likely to kill himself as a function of his magical and/or delusional thought process. The patient in all probability denies any suicidal intent, and the suicide "attempt" of the schizophrenic is often not an attempt at all, but nevertheless lethal. For instance, the authors have expreienced many clients whose delusional system told them they were invincible, or agents of God, etc. These patients often attempted to prove their special powers by threatening to jump out of windows, or jump in front of moving automobiles, or shoot themselves to purge the devil from their heads. The suicide attempt in the schizophrenic is another manifestation of the illness. Therefore, it is almost impossible to ascertain which schizophrenic patient is suicidal, particularly if the patient is actively schizophrenic. Until the schizophrenic symptoms are in remission, it is important to take suicidal precautions with *all* schizophrenic patients.

REFERENCES

American Psychiatric Association (Task Force on Nomenclature Statistics): *Diagnostic and Statistical Manual of Mental Disorders — III Draft.* Washington, D.C., APA, 1978.

Bassuk, Ellen L. and Schoonover, Stephen C.: *The Practitioner's Guide to Psychoactive Drugs.* New York, Plenum Pr, 1977.

Helgason, Tomas: Epidemiology of mental disorder in Iceland. *Acta Psychiatr Scan (Suppl),* 174:1-258, 1964.

Lester, David and Beck, Aaron T.: Suicidal intent, medical lethality of the suicide attempt, and components of depression. *J Clin Psychol,* 31(1):11-12, 1975.

Miles, Charles P.: Conditions predisposing to suicide: a review. *J. Nerv Ment Dis,* 164(4):231-246, 1977.

Paykel, Eugene S.: Life stress, depression and attempted suicide. *J Human Stress,* 2(3):3-12, 1976.

Peck, Michael L.: A young person dies . . . Preventing the Youthful Suicide. In Alan Griffin and David Switzer (Co-chair.): *Preventing the Youthful Suicide.* Symposium presented by Suicide Prevention of Dallas and Southern Methodist University, Dallas, 1977.

Pokorney, Alex D.: Suicide rates in various psychiatric disorders. *J Nerv Ment Dis,* 139:499-506, 1974.

Shneidman, Edwin S., Farberow, Norman L., and Litman, Robert E.: *The Psychology of Suicide.* New York, Science House, 1970.

Thompson, Kay C. and Hendrie, Hugh C.: Environmental stress in primary depressive illness. *Arch Gen Psychiatry,* 26:130-132, 1972.

Winokur, George and Tsuang, Ming: The Iowa 500: Suicide in mania, depression, and schizophrenia. *Am J Psychiatry,* 132(6):650-651, 1975.

Chapter 3

DIAGNOSIS OF THE
SELF-DESTRUCTIVE PERSONALITY

CHAPTER 1 provided an overview concerning which groups of people are more likely to have a higher incidence of suicide. Demographics of suicide are indeed important in the study of suicide, but they are not terribly helpful in the counseling situation when the counselor has to assess the suicidal risk of an individual. This chapter is designed to assist the counselor in assessing the suicidal risk of the client in front of him. The assessment of suicidal risk must often be done "on the spot." Guidelines for the suicidal diagnostic interview are presented to assist the counselor in arriving at as immediate an assessment as possible of the suicidal risk of the client.

EARLY INTERVIEW CUES OF SUICIDAL THOUGHT

Most often when the client makes initial references to suicidal thought they will be veiled and somewhat disguised. It is extremely important for the counselor to pay attention to phrases by the client such as: "Sometimes I just want it to be over"; "I'm tired of the whole thing, I just want to sleep"; "I can't take anymore and I don't see any hope"; or "The world would be better off without me." Any open or veiled reference to suicide must be openly and directly inquired about. If the counselor does not directly deal with this material, it may communicate to the client that the client's feelings are not only frightening to him but also to the counselor. In all likelihood, the client is relieved that it is safe to openly talk about his thoughts of self-destruction once the counselor directly acknowledges the true intent of the veiled communication.

Another interview clue is if the client has been depressed and agitated in previous counseling sessions but suddenly is no longer depressed and is calm. This can often communicate that the client "no longer needs to be depressed" in that he at last has come to the ultimate decision of taking his own life. Once again, the counselor must make direct inquiries of the client as to what is responsible for the sudden change. By direct is meant the counselor stating to the client, "Is this sudden calm brought about by the decision to kill yourself?" It is remarkable how honestly suicidal clients respond to such direct questions when one considers that, up to this point, the client had only been willing to give hints as to his intent.

THE INTERVIEW ASSESSMENT OF SUICIDAL RISK

Once the client has legitimized that he is indeed thinking about suicide, the counseling process must immediately shift direction. At this point, the counselor is obligated to seek the necessary information in order to make an assessment of suicidal risk. This shift may seem disruptive to the "therapeutic process," but it is critical that the counselor know the potential suicidal risk the client presents before further counseling may progress. If there is significant suicidal risk, this becomes the predominant treatment problem and immediately supercedes all other issues. It is critical that the counselor know what issues are the most crucial. Once the suicidal risk is determined, the counselor can either proceed with the previous counseling issues under discussion or move into suicide intervention strategies.

The first question to ask the client in assessing risk is how long has the client had these feelings; the longer the time, the greater the suicidal risk. It is further important for the counselor to inquire as to whether the client has ever had these thoughts or feelings in the past and if he ever acted upon them and how. If the client confirms that these thoughts have occurred in the past, the counselor may further ask what caused the cessation of these thoughts or feelings. This might be helpful for the counselor to use in his treatment of the client. Whatever may have worked in the past for the client, in the termination of these thoughts, may be considered in dealing with the current problems.

The next question, with respect to time, is the frequency and duration of the suicidal thoughts. Are they omnipresent? Do they only occur in certain situations? How often do they occur? Many times a day? A few times per week? Only on certain holidays but always on those holidays? Once a suicidal thought occurs, how long does it last? Fifteen minutes? All day? Naturally the greater the frequency of the thoughts and the greater the duration once they occur, the greater the suicidal risk.

Once frequency and duration are assessed, the counselor should proceed in the evaluation of the suicidal plan or method. This can best be done by merely asking the client to tell you how he plans to kill himself. The more carefully thought through the plan and the more concise the articulation of the plan, the greater the suicidal risk. Many clients make rather vague statements when explaining their plan such as, "I don't know how I'm going to do it, but I'm going to do it." On the other end of the risk continuum the client might state, "I will kill myself before the month is out. I bought a shotgun and have the ammunition. I have picked out the place I will do it; it will be at sunset on the mountain alone." As you can see, this plan is well thought through with a lethal method, a definite time frame within which it will occur, and in a manner that would present very little possibility of rescue. The above client would indeed represent a most serious suicidal risk.

As previously mentioned, a number of other factors must be considered in evaluating a suicidal plan before one can determine the extent of the suicidal risk.

One of these factors is the potential lethality of the method. A method that would have low lethality might be one in which the client suggests that he intends to take his life by slashing his wrists, or ingesting less than fifteen aspirins. Neuringer (1974) in explaining his assessment of the lethality of method, discusses it in the context of how reversible the method is in attempting to save the client's life once he has attempted suicide. The above examples represent in Neuringer's framework a "completely reversible" method. He would define as a "Probable and Expected Reversibility of Method" the following kinds of attempts: ingestion of ten or more tranquilizers, or stimulants, or the cutting of the wrists to require vessel and/or tendon repair. Even more lethal attempts would be seen in his "Questionable Reversibility of Method" to include the ingestion of ten or more prescription sleeping medication, poisons, or large amounts or combinations of several drugs or narcotics. The next category is "Improbable and Unexpected Reversibility of Method." This category would include plans to attempt to drown oneself, carbon monoxide suffocation, attempts at gas suffocation, deep cuts to the throat, or jumping from a place less than twenty feet in elevation. Finally the most lethal group of methods of suicide attempt that he defines is "Remote or No Chance for Reversibility of Method." This classification would include the following types of attempts: gunshot in vital area, jumping from a place more than twenty feet high, or hanging. Again, the more lethal the proposed method the client is contemplating the greater the suicidal risk.

Another factor to be evaluated in the client's plan is the likelihood of rescue. Is the attempt likely to take place in a public place using a low to moderately lethal method? In this case the client is providing for himself a high probabilty of life-saving intervention. Or does the client intend to take a large dose of sleeping pills in a remote place? Here the method is probably lethal and it is unlikely that the client would be discovered in time to save his life. An even more threatening plan with respect to the likelihood of intervention would be the jumping off a high precipice in a desolate area. Here the client has made sure that he has thwarted all attempts at rescue.

The counselor must be very careful in assessing suicidal risk and must not rely on the client's unconscious judgment as to whether there will be rescue. It has been the misfortune of too many women to have died because of a miscalculation in the arrival times of their husbands. They take sleeping pills at 4:15 PM knowing full well that their husband is always home by 5 o'clock, but this time his car broke down on the freeway. Perhaps these women did not really intend to kill themselves, nevertheless they are dead.

The whole concept of the probability of intervention in suicide attempts is an interesting one. There are some who contend that most people who kill themselves are ambivalent about their suicidal act right up until the moment of their death. Therefore, most suicidal plans have at least an element of the probability of being rescued although unfortunately often a small one.

Time frame is also an important consideration in evaluating suicidal risk. The more specific and more proximate the intended suicide is to the present, the greater the suicidal risk. The client who states that this is his last day alive is of course a most grave immediate risk. The client who states he will be dead before a given date would be a lesser suicidal risk, and even less a risk, the further the specified date is from the present. Again, however, the counselor is urged to view client's time frames for self-demise with extreme caution in that events often occur which change or speed up the time frame.

OTHER DIAGNOSTIC CUES IN
ASCERTAINING SUICIDAL POTENTIAL

Doctor Calvin Frederick in a recent suicide symposium (Preventing the Youthful Suicide, 1977) presents the suicidal individual as experiencing "Haplessness, hopelessness, and helplessness." He states that these feelings are strong indications of suicide potential. Haplessness is the belief of the client that he has been victimized by society. He perceives that everything that could go wrong in his life has gone wrong. This allows the client to displace the source of the anguish external to the client. In its most extreme forms these feelings take on a paranoid quality in that the client feels people are out to get him.

Hopelessness is experienced by the client in that he cannot see "any light at the end of the tunnel." The client feels there is no hope and therefore there is no commitment to living. The client believes that, if anything, matters will only get worse.

Helplessness is the client's belief of being powerless. The client is convinced that no matter what he does, it will not work in alleviating the anguish. It abdicates the client from being responsible for his actions in that he has declared he is helpless.

These feelings occur in virtually all suicidal clients. The more the client experiences these feelings the more likely suicide becomes an option. The recognition of these feelings by the counselor and the subsequent pointing out of the same by the counselor to the client can provide the beginnings of an intervention strategy. Each of these feelings and beliefs and, perhaps more importantly, the assumptions behind them can be openly challenged by the counselor. Each of these feelings is predicated upon irrational and unreasonable thought. The open challenge of these assumptions can give the counselor direction in dealing with the client. It is important for the counselor to point out that we are all responsible for our actions, that we can take action to offset the impact of our past deeds, and that we are victims of our culture only to the extent we allow ourselves to be.

Still other clues to suicide would be the client who is anxious, irritable, and panicky. These result in the client feeling he is losing control (Lettieri, 1974; Lester, 1967). Farberow and McEvoy (1966) found people who had killed themselves to have also exhibited sleeplessness, agitation, nervousness, worries, and marked anxiety and depression. All of these cues in the presence of a suicide plan increase the gravity of the suicidal risk even if the plan is of relatively low lethality.

Another factor which has been shown to be correlated with suicide is a family history of suicide, particularly if the mother died by her own hand (Worden, 1972).

The problem of insomnia deserves further comment. Of course, insomnia is an indication of depression. Most depressed people have some difficulty with insomnia. But even though they may have some difficulty either in falling asleep or in maintaining sleep, they nevertheless typically report having some sleep during the night. What is particularly dangerous is the client who reports not having any sleep for the last two or three days. This is critical in two respects. First, it could well be an indication that the client is in the early stages of an acute psychotic episode of either manic or schizophrenic type. Perhaps more dangerous, the client is also likely to be in acute severe psychic anguish, exhausted, irritable, and consequently the consideration of suicide might represent an end to this terrible turmoil.

Another variable often mentioned in suicide assessment is that of recent loss (Ganzler, 1967; Farber, 1968), particularly losses within the last six months. Significant loss may be the death of a loved one, separation, divorce, or the loss of position, such as a job, resulting in loss of self-esteem. The more grievous the loss and the more central the lost object, event, or person was to the client, the greater the contribution to suicidal risk.

Depression, as has been discussed earlier, is often a partner of suicidal intent. In assessing suicidal risk it is also important for the counselor to place some importance as to whether the client "feels better" at the end of the counseling session. The clients who have most often concerned us in our practice are those who do not feel better towards the end of the session. A further point to consider in evaluating the depressed suicidal client is whether the client is capable of smiling. It is recommended that the counselor on some occasion in the counseling interview say something that is humorous. If the client is incapable of smiling, even if it is for nothing else than acknowledging the counselor's attempt at humor, it may be an indication of the depth of the depression. Another indication of the depth of the depression is if the client has ceased performing those activities that previously had brought him pleasure, such as giving up hobbies, regular attendance at sporting events, etc.

When it is apparent that the client is "putting his house in order," this is to be taken as a serious suicidal sign. Putting one's house in order may include the client seeing that there is ready access to his important papers, contact with significant others to say goodbye, giving away prized possessions (not things that were necessarily of great monetary worth), and making sure his will is in order.

Another point for the counselor to consider is references to the future. Does the client speak in the future tense? Can he tell you what both his vocational and personal plans are for the future? The fewer future referrants, the greater the possibility the client is thinking of suicide. If the client makes no reference to the future, the counselor should inquire as to the client's future plans. If he has none, this may be an indication of suicidal potential.

THE SUICIDAL CRISIS

Much has been written concerning suicide and suicide intervention. However, very little has been available in assisting the counselor in determining how long a client remains acutely suicidal and what the critical phases are during the time the client is actively considering suicide.

A suicidal crisis may last for months, or in the case of the chronically suicidal individual, it may be a constant state. However, in the majority of suicidal individuals the suicidal crisis is usually about six weeks. During the first week there is a high risk of suicide. At this time the counselor must intervene for the client so that others know the gravity of the client's problems. Suicidal precautions must be taken by the counselor in an attempt to ensure the protection of the client. This may include consideration of hospitalization, an evaluation for medication, or informing family members or clergy to be supportive and not leave the client alone. During the week, the counselor should have frequent contact with the client. If the counselor can prevent the client from an attempt or gesture during the first week, he will have accomplished a significant feat.

During the following two weeks the client will probably still talk about his suicidal thoughts but is less likely to act upon them. The counselor may still have to see the client two or three times a week during this phase of the suicidal crisis. The counselor will probably be focusing on what the client may do to start asserting control over his existence.

The next crescendo of suicidal risk is likely to occur when the client starts feeling less depressed. The last two weeks of this six-week cycle are perhaps the most critical. In this phase the client in all likelihood has shown signs of improvement. He probably is not as depressed. Medications, if they had been prescribed, are likely to start having positive effects. If the client had been hospitalized during the first week of the crisis, he in all probability would have now been discharged. It is imperative that the counselor not let up his guard in the face of this improvement, for now the client has new energy and clearer thoughts but yet may be suicidal. He has all the ingredients in this situation to successfully complete his suicidal wishes.

Of course, there is a great deal of variability of the above time sequence. It is merely a statement of "averages," which is perhaps dangerous in looking at any given individual. Further, the above does not take into consideration those people who are chronically suicidal. The chronically suicidal merely moves from one suicidal crisis to the next with little time intervening from cycle to cycle.

Another group which does not fit into "cycles of crisis" are the psychotic, particularly schizophrenics. The schizophrenic is a constant potential suicidal risk and is particularly frustrating to the counselor in that the degree of risk at any point in time is almost impossible to ascertain, since the schizophrenic's referrants to suicide, if present at all, are usually terribly abstract. Yet, it is this very group that exhibits the most lethal attempts when they do try to kill themselves (Dorpat and Boswell, 1963; Lester, 1970). For example, the schizophrenic may talk about seriously cutting himself to let the devil out of his blood or threaten to take poison to prove he has special protection from God.

GESTURE VERSUS ATTEMPT

Diagnostically, it is often fairly easy to establish whether a suicidal act had been a gesture or one that was an actual attempt at self-murder. Two factors are taken into consideration in determining if a suicidal act was a gesture. The first is the lethality of the method. Those attempts that would be characterized as being of low lethality with respect to method would most likely be classified by having a high probability of intervention or rescue. Most gestures are of both low lethality of method and have high probability of rescue.

Although differentiating attempt from gesture may be of important psychological consequence for the counselor in evaluating the client, it has little practical meaning with respect to suicide intervention. A gesture must be treated with the same seriousness as an attempt. The suicidal gesture is a desperate cry for help. If it is dismissed as being manipulative or hysterical, the risk of a legitimate attempt dramatically increases. Worden (1976) points out that with clients with no psychiatric history prior to their first suicidal attempt, if they subsequently received treatment then made a second attempt, it would be of lower lethality. With those clients who did not receive treatment after the first attempt, the second attempt was likely to be of greater lethality.

In practice, then, differentiating a suicidal attempt from a suicidal gesture is academic in that in practice they must be dealt with in an equally serious manner.

REFERENCES

Dorpat, Theodore L. and Boswell, John W.: An evaluation of suicidal intent in suicide attemptors. *Compr Psychiatry, 4*:117-125, 1963.

Farber, Maurice L.: *Theory of Suicide.* New York, Funk & W, 1968.

Farberow, Norman and McEvoy, Theodore: Suicide among patients with diagnoses of anxiety reaction or depressive reaction in general medical and surgical hospitals. *J Abnorm Psychol, 71*:287-299, 1966.

Frederick, Calvin J.: Advances in suicidology. In Alan Griffin and David Switzer (Co-chair.): *Preventing the Youthful Suicide.* Symposium presented by Suicide Prevention of Dallas and Southern Methodist University, Dallas, 1977.

Ganzler, Sidney: Some interpersonal and social dimensions of suicidal behavior. *Dissertation Abstracts, 28(3-B)*:1192-1193, 1967.

Lester, David: Suicide as an aggressive act. *J. Psychol, 66*:47-50, 1967.

Lester, David: Factors affecting choice of method of suicide. *J Clin Psychol, 26(5)*:437, 1970.

Lettieri, Dan J.: Research issues in developing prediction scales. In Neuringer, Charles: *Psychological Assessment of Suicidal Risk.* Springfield, Thomas, 1974.

Worden, J. William: Lethality factors and the suicide attempt. In Neuringer, Charles: *Psychological Assessment of Suicidal Risk.* Springfield,

Thomas, 1974.

SUGGESTED READINGS

Anderson, Dorothy B. and McClean, Lenora J. (Eds.): *Identifying Suicide Potential.* New York, Behavioral Pubns, 1969.

Beck, Aaron T., Resnik, H. L. P., and Lettieri, Dan J. (Eds.): *The Prediction of Suicide.* Bowie, Md, Charles, 1974.

Kiev, Ari: *The Suicidal Patient: Recognition and Management.* Chicago, Nelson-Hall, 1977.

Chapter 4

COUNSELING WITH THE SUICIDAL CLIENT

COUNSELING with the suicidal individual is a very complex task with many factors affecting the counselor and client, as well as the process. Each client is unique and the problems presented are different; consequently, counseling plans and strategies will vary from client to client. It is our intent in this chapter to examine general treatment considerations which apply to the broad range of self-destructive clients.

GENERAL CONSIDERATIONS

All of the basic counseling skills are essential to work with the suicidal. Such skills as active listening, demonstrating empathy, paraphrasing, reflection, interpretation, and summarization are always an integral part of the process. There are a number of other skills and treatment considerations which are especially important in working with people who are considering suicide.

Making Contact

Clients who are potentially self-destructive are, in many ways, much different from all other types of clients. The essential difference is that human life is at stake. Because of the life-threatening nature of the problem, time is of the essence. A working relationship must be quickly established in order that the destructive processes be brought under control.

The essential first step is making the person-to-person contact with the client. He must know that he is talking with a person who is actively interested in his well-being.

Contact can be established in many ways: verbally, nonverbally, subtly, straightforward, directly, personally, or through others. The purpose of contact is to reduce, and eventually stop, self-destructive acts and to assist the client in developing new and more constructive means of adjustment. Words, voice tone, and eye contact are some of the primary means of contact; somehow the client must be made to hear what the counselor is saying, and then the client must go on to really understand what is being said. Touch may well accompany the counselor's words. Physical contact can give comfort as well as a sense of security to the suicidal individual. For many clients an indirect approach is essential. Gradually, over an extended period of time, the counselor works with the individual to help him understand his situation and cope with it. For others a direct, straightforward confrontation as to their actions and the possible consequences can stop the destructive process. Some clients work best when involved in a face-to-face dialogue with their counselor. Others feel more comfortable if some family member or trusted friend is actively involved with them in the counseling process. ˜

Treatment approaches must be creatively designed for each client. The talents of the therapist must be brought to bear upon the special and individual needs of every client; a personalized approach is essential to the success of counseling. As initial contact is made, the counselor is continuously assessing the client and making decisions as to the method of procedure.

Showing Understanding

Many suicidal individuals believe they are not understood. They view their world from a solitary position and think no one else can gain a sense of their reality. Clients also doubt that anyone else has ever experienced the feelings they have. The experience of aloneness is very depressing and pessimistic. To have someone show, in any fashion, that they either do understand or are willing to work hard at understanding is very important to the suicidal individual.

Counselors who engage in active listening with their clients will have a good chance of making firm, constructive contact.

By paying attention to the full range of what the client has to say, the counselor is in a very good position to demonstrate a high level of understanding. To achieve this level of understanding, the counselor must listen to such things as voice quality, language, tone, volume, and pauses, as well as the content of what is being said. The isolation of a client begins to change as he sees and hears another person struggle to understand what he is thinking and feeling. The client no longer feels quite so alone, and begins to feel understood.

Establishing Hope

As the client senses that someone understands, even a little, it is easier to believe that there is hope in that the barriers of isolation are beginning to break down. Explicitly and implicitly the counselor is attempting to demonstrate to the client that his problems can be resolved in the counseling process. No matter how bad things may seem, there is still hope for positive change. Clients who are in the depths of despair must be shown that they can expect to improve and get better. Even though the first appeal for hope is to the intellect of the client, it is hoped it will eventually be internalized into the client's feelings. Reassurance is very important to this sense of well-being. Being told "While it may take some time to get better, you can expect to feel progressively more able to cope with your life situation" can reaffirm the sense of hope which is desperately needed.

The counselor can directly acknowledge that being depressed and having thoughts of suicide is a very uncomfortable and frightening position, but depression itself is not lethal. The counselor can then go on to reassure the client that he can learn how to keep his depression and suicidal thoughts from getting worse, and further that these feelings will be reduced and eventually dissipate completely. Another tactic involves the counselor giving permission to the client to have suicidal thoughts and to reassure him that such thoughts in and of themselves are not dangerous. The counselor then goes on to reassure the client that the counselor is confident that the client will not act out on such thoughts. The client must know that effective treatment can go on even though suicidal thoughts are happening. As the client feels more hopeful, impulsive, self-destructive actions become less likely.

Permission, Protection, and Potency

The counselor's use of Permission, Protection, and Potency are critical to the success of counseling the suicidal client. Permission refers to the concept that the client must know it is all right or that it is appropriate to change. Some clients do not believe that they are capable of doing things differently in their lives; they think they are destined to be the way they are. The counselor can let them know that change is not only possible but probable, even though at this time it is difficult for the client to accept this.

Protection refers to the process of letting the client know that he is not alone while the course of constructive changes is taking place. The counselor will always be there to assist and sometimes shield the client during growth. Being in a state of developmental change is very often a frightening and vulnerable experience. Knowing that protection from the counselor is available is a steadying factor, and the counselor becomes the ally of change in the client.

Potency refers to the power of the counselor as felt by the client which allows the counselor to facilitate change. The client must trust the counselor and sense this available strength. Potency develops over time and is manifested as credibility. It is based on several factors. For some clients, the counselor's title adds to the potency. For others knowing that the counselor is understanding and has good suggestions can increase credibility.

Jointly the three Ps add substance to the work of the counselor.

Action Plans

Contact, understanding, hope, and the three Ps are all involved in the initial phases of any treatment plan. As time progresses, the steps of the plan are specifically outlined for the client and the counselor as a function of mutual negotiation. Significant others such as friends, family, or other helping agencies will be integrated into the planning process as is appropriate. Treatment schedules, time lines for action steps, and contingency plans will evolve during the counseling process. As the client works with the counselor, problems will be identified and steps for their solution will be developed. This process entails the clarification of thought and feeling and sorting out of alternatives. The completion of the process results in the formulation of specific behavioral change contracts. Gradually, a framework for life will be rebuilt by the client and counselor working as a team.

Form of Treatment

Counseling with the suicidal individual may take many forms. In early stages of treatment, individual counseling is usually initiated. Clients during crisis are often more reachable if the incidence of outside stimuli is kept to a minimum. Being seen in a group or with his family, at this early stage, may be too complex; the client might not be able to process all of the information coming from so many people.

The new client is, for the most part, an unknown entity. No one is certain how the client got to the point of crisis, nor is it certain what kinds of events or feelings might accelerate the self-destructive process. Consequently, each client must be treated as an individual and the counselor must avoid the trap of feeling that since he has dealt with suicidal crises in the past, that which has worked in the past is what must be done in the present. As an information base is developed concerning the individual client, and a treatment plan is formulated, other methods of intervention can be introduced at appropriate times. This might include group treatment which will serve to let the client know he is not alone in his feelings. This can be very helpful to the person who once thought no one else could have ever experienced what he is experiencing. Group counseling also offers a broad-based support system to the client:

knowing that others care and are willing to help is reassuring.

Incorporating the family into therapy is another useful modality. Significant others in the client's life can be brought into the working counseling situation. Confusion, misunderstanding, and constructive steps for future interaction can be discussed among all those involved with the client. A treatment plan which attacks the problem from as many positions as possible has the highest chance of success.

CLIENT VARIABLES

Each client has unique characteristics and symptoms which must be dealt with in the counseling process. There are, however, a number of commonalities of symptoms which are frequently found among individuals who are self-destructive. We will enumerate a number of these and discuss ways in which they may be treated.

Ambivalence

The individual considering suicide as an option is usually ambivalent. His thoughts vacillate between wanting to kill himself and wanting to stay alive. This indecision is an important key to any intervention. The counselor can make a great deal of headway and at the same time avoid many pitfalls into therapy by immediately helping the client recognize this vacillation. This is most dramatically shown by the highly suicidal client who has somehow made it to the counselor's office or to the emergency room. In spite of the inner push toward self-destruction, the client is yet still alive. By being there with you the client, with his words and behavior, is saying very clearly that he wants to live.

In the initial phase of counseling, the counselor must clearly show the client that he sees and understands both elements. It is essential that the counselor sense both the pulse of life and the drive toward death. As the relationship is more firmly established, the counselor can encourage the client to stay in touch with and talk from that part which is life-sustaining. This method of responding to and nurturing the life force allows the course of counseling to follow a positive, constructive track. In some instances the counselor can even refuse to talk with the negative, death-considering part of the client. This is a potent control of the direction of counseling. It is from the life-sustaining side that the client can work at identifying stresses and developing alternatives for life. The drive toward death is diminished as hope is developed within the client. Of course, the counselor has to recognize the potential danger in this tack of ignoring the suicidal feelings which may push the client away. There must be a delicate balance.

Another direction to take with the ambivalent suicidal individual is to have him identify which specific part of himself he is trying to destroy. In some instances death is used as a means of getting rid of only one feature of an otherwise "good" individual. The client's feelings of guilt, envy, hate, or physical disfigurement may be so overwhelming that he can think of no means other than total destruction as a solution. This situation allows the counselor to work with the client in helping him see the many other parts of his physical and emotional being; positive values can be placed on these other aspects. Creatively, the counselor can help the client find alternative methods to deal with the one or more painful, hated, or despicable aspects. The client can be shown that the sum of his being is much greater than just one or more of his parts.

As the counselor openly talks about the suicidal situation with the client, some of the fearfulness is removed. It is easily seen by the client that he is no longer alone; the counselor is providing a potent life-sustaining force by being willing to be there with the client. The confusion and turmoil created by the conflict between the life and death aspects begins to abate as the client begins to more carefully consider his situation.

Motive

Usually there is no single reason why an individual chooses death as an option. This decision is a complicated one based on many factors. Consequently, the question "WHY?" is frequently unanswerable, especially if a precise answer is wanted. In working with the suicidal, it is important not to fall into the trap of attempting to find that one special cause. Consider the person's life to be similar to a jigsaw puzzle, and you are working with him in an attempt to bring some sort of order to the many pieces. It will become clear that, as you work, there will be many holes in the puzzle because many of the pieces or reasons for various actions are just not available. Do not be discouraged by this fact and do not let the client be discouraged. Realize that even a vague outline or form to the picture is much more than the client had before he started counseling. However, the motive or motives behind suicidal thoughts and acts are important in the reeducation of the client. Some sense of understanding as to motive is a reasonable goal in counseling.

For some, suicide is an overtly hostile act or an expression of anger. It is a weapon directed at those who are left behind. "They'll be sorry" is a frequent statement from the suicidal. Helping the client identify who "they" are and finding out exactly what is wanted from "them" can be an important piece of information. Constructively, this data could be used to determine less destructive means to get what is really wanted. New ways of expressing anger might be taught.

Attempting to induce guilt in others may be a motive for suicide. The client believes that his family will be totally and forever upset by his death. In this situation, the anger is not so clear. The use of fantasy is one way to intervene in situations of this type. The client can be asked to view in his mind's eye how his family will react at hearing of his death; how they will be at the funeral; how they will be three months, six months, a year, and two years later. Most often the client, with the creative and directive help of the counselor, will see that the family disruption will not be long-lasting. Their lives will go on much as before his death. The drama and impact, at the moment, of suicide will soon be lost over time. With this bit of information, the client can be helped to discover more constructive ways to be impactful upon family members.

Suicidal activity is often the way to express hopelessness and helplessness. This desperate method of attracting attention is resorted to when the client can find no other way of coping or when he believes that others do not perceive, in any way, his terrible life situation. From the beginning, clients must be taught new ways of relating to the significant others in their life. The client can be taught how to identify personal needs and then go on to express these needs to others. If some individuals are not in a position to respond to these needs, the client must learn how to go to others to find self-satisfaction.

It is possible that suicidal behavior may be designed as a way to get recognition. Everyone needs recognition; if we do not get positive recognition, we will seek out negative. Anything will be done to avoid being ignored. As the client sees this as being one of the reasons for his behavior, he can be taught how to identify and carry out new means of getting positive recognition.

The use of suicidal threats to get attention may become habitual. The client in this case has learned that his "cry for help" will usually get a response from those people in his life. From a learning point of view, anything that has once been learned can be unlearned. The question "How else can you get what you want?" can move the client to examine new behaviors that will achieve the same end in a healthy manner.

Many suicidal individuals have, at some point in their developmental history, either been literally or figuratively abandoned. Their parents may have died when they were small or for some reason they might have been placed in foster homes or with relatives. Perhaps, the client may fear that unless he acts in a certain way he will be abandoned. The impact of this situation is such that the client grows to believe that there is something intrinsically wrong with him. He is so bad or so inadequate that no one wants him; he does not deserve to keep on living. Suicide can then become a viable option. Counseling makes it possible for the client to reassess personal worth and realize that he does deserve to live. For many clients, the logical discussion of the situation is enough of a motivator to eliminate suicide as a coping mechanism. Here, the object of attack for the counselor is the "illogical" thoughts and assumptions of the client.

In summation, suicide may also be seen as a means of communication. There are many possibilities as to what the client is trying to say to specific individuals, groups, or the world in general. A death attempt may be a confession or may mean, "I'm sorry," "They'll be sorry," "I hate you," "There is no hope," or "Help me." The counselor can assist the client to find possible motives by asking the proper questions. Asking, "What are you trying to say by killing yourself?", "Whom are you speaking to?", or "How else could you say that?" coupled with "How should they change?" can assist the client to find new ways of reaching others. This type of clarification also helps the client reach himself. He now has a chance to hear himself clearly and speak out to others in a direct fashion.

Suicide may be a way to adapt, to handle a current stressful situation. By seeking clarification and a complete description and understanding of the present problem, the counselor assists the client to find new ways of adjusting. The counselor might ask, "How is it that you are so helpless to bring about change in a way other than suicide?" This helps the client think through how he got into such a situation in the first place. The implied message is that the client is not really helpless and can do something more constructive in dealing with the immediate problem.

Agitation

The agitated client is especially dangerous. Agitation may be expressed in many ways. Rapid speech, many changes of topic, finger twisting or hand wringing, tremors, an inability to sit still, and pacing are a few of the indications of high energy. The client may talk openly about his discomfort because it is so unsettling. This type of individual must be attended to with consistency and control. It is very important for the counselor to be calm, reassuring, and willing to take an active part in the interaction. For some clients who are in the early stages of agitation, a simple instruction to "Stop agitating" or "I want you to *think* about what is happening" may be enough to stop any escalation of behavior. Another possibility would be for the client to lean back and take deep breaths and then to exhale slowly. It is essential that the counselor be willing to stay with the client until the agitation has been reduced. The client should never be left alone in a room to cool off and collect himself. As the behaviors increase, most clients feel more and more out of control, and being alone is a frightening and intolerable situation. In the extreme instances, medications could be used to calm the client. Quick action is essential to provide firm, controlling protection.

When agitation is combined with severe depression, the risk for the safety of the client increases. This individual is very impulsive because of the extreme level of discomfort and he wants relief immediately. Consequently, suicide becomes especially appealing. The use of medication to calm the client is often indicated in these instances. Medication offers an immediate reduction of the agitation and impulsiveness. Family and friends are very important resources in the treatment of these clients. The significant others can be recruited to spend time with the client so he will not be alone and consequently will be less likely to act out impulsively. The counselor must be willing to be very directive and establish guidelines for the family and for the client. For example, if the family members are to stay with the client, they need to know this means *all* the time; both the client and the family need to be informed clearly of the reasons for this procedure.

Retarded Depression

The client who suffers from this symptom requires a different treatment plan than the agitated depressive. These individuals most often are depressed for long periods of time; consequently, it is very easy for family members to become numb, immune, or insensitive to his bad feelings. Both the counselor and the family must work at keeping in touch with the client's feelings and not ignore any change, no matter how small. Being in tune with the client is especially important as the depression begins to lift and he has more energy; it is at this point that the client might well have enough energy to kill himself. Continuity and consistency of treatment is very important for the client of this type. As the working through process advances, it is essential not to move too slowly nor too quickly. Resolution of problems must be carefully paced and outcomes of behavior changes monitored. Termination of the counseling relationship needs to be carefully planned for and discussed well in advance. It is especially important not to terminate too soon; the client must be ready to go out on his own without the support of the counselor.

The Suicidal Schizophrenic

Treatment of the schizophrenic who is demonstrating self-destructive thoughts or behavior is especially difficult. Individuals of this nature are very unpredictable due to the nature of the primary disorder, the schizophrenia. The suicidal aspects are secondary, and even though important to work with in treatment, the major treatment focus must be on the schizophrenia. Therefore, the use of medication is essential to keep some level of control on the disturbed thought processes. During times of increased suicidal thinking, hospitalization for the client's safety is the best treatment plan. At best, the prognosis for these clients is poor.

Impulse Control

Impulse control is a critical issue in counseling. Many suicidal clients feel almost totally out of control, and they have very little confidence in their ability to exert self-control. They sometimes think they *have to* act out, that they have no other choice. This faulty thinking must be dealt with immediately. For some it is as simple as telling them that they do not have to put into action everything they think. Giving them permission to screen their thoughts and to keep them separate from action may be all that it takes to help them regain control.

Impulsivity can also be dealt with in an educational fashion; the client can be taught possible alternative actions that can be used instead of impulsive, destructive acts. For the extremely impulsive client, the first step is to teach him that he must get help when he begins to feel he is losing control. He must know to whom he can turn for assistance and how he should go about doing it. The counselor should teach him how to get in touch with a crisis phone line, call the police, or go to the local hospital emergency room. He also needs to know how to explain his critical life situation to another person. Since many emergency room services are overrun by hysterical demanding patients, the truly dangerous client must be able to demand protection in time of high need.

Ventilation of Emotion and Physical Energy

The emotionally charged individual develops a reserve of physical energy. Each client must find ways to allow for a constructive discharge of both the emotional and physical energy. The protective atmosphere of the therapy setting is an excellent medium in which to aid the client in this discharge. The energized client might be asked to, first, identify the individual, thing, or situation to which he is reacting. Second, the message or demand that the client really wants to be expressed is clarified. With the aid of the counselor, the client then finds a more constructive way to tell or ask for what is needed. The use of fantasy is especially helpful in this situation. The client may fantasize the person to whom he wants to make a demand, and the counselor assists him in expressing verbally to that individual; the actual acting out of the fantasy is important. If anger is the base emotion, the pounding of pillows while expressing the demand also helps drain off and reduce to controllable limits the emotional and physical energy. After the expression, the client must be assisted in thinking through the experience and determining ways the energy build-up could have been prevented or developing new ways of handling similar events in the future. It is important to combine the aspects of thought, emotion, and eventual behavior change. One without the other prevents the complete resolution of the situation.

For release of physical energy between counseling sessions,

there are many possibilities for the client. Jogging, house cleaning, weight lifting, hitting a heavy punching bag, yard work, and physical exercises are just a few. One creative client saved all of the empty food cans and when she felt energy build up, she would take them into the garage and jump on them until they were all flat. Just the release of physical energy helped her control her destructive feelings. Clients can be taught to develop their own special program for constructive channeling of energy.

Mind Racing

Many clients experience discomfort because of the rapidity of their thinking, or because they focus on one especially disconcerting thought. Feelings of helplessness and despair can quickly escalate as the client is unable to change the focus or pace of the thought process. The concept of thought stopping may be helpful in this instance. The concept is taught during the therapy hour and sets of practice sessions are developed. The client is told to sit back in the chair with his eyes closed and begin to think of a common disturbing thought. When the thought is firmly in mind, the client is to signal by lifting one finger. The therapist then leans close to the client and shouts *STOP!!* The typical pattern is for the client to jump and be extremely startled. When asked what happened to his troublesome thought, he will most likely respond that he is no longer thinking of it. The client is then logically and systematically taught how he can, in his own mind, tell himself to stop thinking a bothersome thought. Practice sessions in the therapy setting help the client move from the vocal to the subvocal command. He is then trained to go on to some new activity after he has interrupted his disturbing train of thought. As the technique is firmly established, the next step is taken. The client is taught that mind racing or rumination on a single topic is actually a signal that something else is happening in his life which is upsetting. He is taught to look logically and rationally at his current surroundings and into the recent past or near future to see if he can determine what there is to be upset about. The client is taught to pay attention to himself and take effective action in response to situations rather than become overwhelmed by troublesome thoughts.

Overgeneralizing

Self-destructive individuals, as well as other clients, frequently overgeneralize. It is very difficult for them to differentiate ideas from facts and to know when they are making assumptions. This situation engenders a very distorted and incomplete view of reality. The counselor is in a good position to assist the client to be more specific and thereby clarify reality. Questions from the counselor like, "What . . . ?", "How . . . ?", "When . . . ?", "In what manner . . . ?", and "Who . . . ?", can assist the client to specify and become less vague. A statement such as "People hate me" is followed by a counselor response of "Which people hate you?" "There is nothing to live for" is responded to by "How have you determined that?"

The client is also encouraged to check out his observations and validate his basic premises. He can be taught how to check out his perceptions with the people in his life. The concept of feedback can be introduced and the client instructed how to ask for and give accurate responses. The counselor is continually attempting to make certain that the client's view of the world is as accurate as possible.

Negativism

It is very common for suicidal individuals to be very negative in their thoughts and feelings. From their point of view there are very few positive aspects to their life. It is as if they completely overlook the good things that are going on in the world of which they are a part. Consequently, the thought of suicide is even more appealing since there is very little positive cause to live.

The task of the counselor in this situation becomes one of forcing the client to recognize what positive elements are in operation in his life. If the client is certain that there is nothing positive currently going on, then the question "What positive things would you like to see in your life?" can be asked. As these items are listed, the counselor can move on to help the client determine ways in which these things can be implemented and developed.

It is not unusual for the acutely depressed and suicidal client to develop feelings of guilt during the course of counseling because (in his eyes) he is not getting well fast enough. The sense of hopelessness may also increase because so many of the symptoms are not eliminated immediately. It is at this point that the client might get desperate and discouraged, thinking "Here I am in counseling and I am not getting better; I must be a hopeless case." This is where the counselor must carefully explain and reexplain that it takes time to get well, and the client must have enough trust in the counselor to stick with the plan. Some clients who are put on medicine for their depression have an almost magical expectation that all will now be better. This is usually not the case because antidepressant medicine takes more than a few days to have any real effect. Realistic expectations must be explained to the client. Clients can be taught how to view their progress. For most, day-to-day gains are not evident; when they are taught to look back to what they were like when they first started counseling as compared to how they are some weeks or months into the process, the gains and changes are more evident and a positive outlook is easier to maintain.

Not Taking Responsibility

For many clients a life-style has developed which revolves around a refusal to accept responsibility for their actions. Clues to this are found in the way they talk, the words that are a regular part of their vocabulary. The impact of this style is on the level of action; they are stuck, immobilized.

Yes, but	It isn't fair	No, but . . . .
If only	But aren't we all .	I'll try . . . .

What if	I know, but	Maybe...........
I can't.......	I don't know	Others don't .....

When these patterns are heard, the passive nature of the client must be confronted. The client must be shown how this style of speech reinforces personal ineptness and "stuckness." If the client is to take charge of his life, then it is essential that passivity be given up and responsible action taken. The counselor can assist in this process by helping the client see what is being gained by being passive and irresponsible. Another direction that may be fruitful is that of determining how the client learned this style of behavior. As insight is gained, it becomes easier to discard nonproductive behavior. However, the search for insight can be carried too far. Some clients believe that they must know *WHY* they are the way they are before they can be responsible and effectively change their behavior. This is just not true. Although it may be nice to know the whys, a client can take responsible action and change behavior without ever knowing why. It is up to the counselor to find the balance for each client between the need for insight and the responsible change of behavior.

Needing To Save Face

For some individuals, pride is a very powerful component of their personality. It can be a driving force for the client that he always does what he says he will do. In these instances, where the client has made a firm and even public decision that he will kill himself, the counselor must be creative in establishing ways in which the client can change his mind without seeming to go back on his word. Options as to all possible decisions must be thoroughly discussed. It must be clear to the client that he is never really backed into a corner; he can always get out gracefully. Here the Potency of the counselor can enable giving a Permission that it is acceptable to change one's mind. The logical, rational situation of "making a mistake" can be discussed. Some clients have never been taught that it is all right to make mistakes. In as many ways as possible, the rigidity of the client is replaced with a more flexible approach to life.

Maintaining Suicide as an Option

It is not uncommon for the suicidal individual, for long periods of his life, to hold the idea that if things get too bad he can always end his life. This always gives him an out; if nothing else worked he could die. In effect, he will never run out of mechanisms by which he can cope with stress. If the client suddenly gives serious thought to giving up the option of suicide, there can be a huge void in the defense system. Realization of this void can keep some clients from making a decision to give up suicide as an option. The counselor must be certain to work with the client to identify and *fully develop* alternative coping systems. All possibilities must be discussed and clarified before the client can be allowed to go out on his own. The work must not be stopped too soon. It can often be reassuring to this type of client that he always had the possibility of suicide open to him in the future. You, as the counselor, are merely asking that he defer this option until the counseling process is tried, since suicide is irrevocable.

Not Having Permission to Live

The desire to die can be a very powerful force. For some clients, this force has been part of their existence for many years. In fact, they have learned it from the parental figures in their childhood and adolescence. Somehow the client has decided that he should either never have been born or that he does not have the right to continue to live. He has never internalized the idea that he is all right and that he should stay alive. No one has told him implicitly or explicitly that he should live. It is also at this juncture that the Potency of the counselor is so very important. In the time of suicidal crisis to hear the words, "I want you to stay alive!" can have a very important impact on the client. To have someone say directly to him that "It is OK for you to keep on living" can be a turning point. As the relationship between the counselor and the client grows, these

Permissions become even more important.

Redecisions

Life-styles develop over many years. There is a tremendous investment in maintaining the course that has been set. In fact, these patterns are so deep seated that many clients believe that it is impossible for them to change in any significant fashion. The individual in crisis may acknowledge that it is possible to get through the crisis, but he does not really believe that any lasting impact or major change in life is possible. Education of the client is very important at this point. The counselor is in a position to show the client that change is possible because the client has the power to make new decisions. No matter what the circumstances of earlier influences or decisions, the client has the power within himself to reevaluate the situation and consequently redecide. The client can be willful and take new responsibility for his direction. As the client accepts this new outlook on life, the counselor assists by teaching new problem-solving skills or new relationship skills.

COUNSELOR VARIABLES

The major attributes of the counselor, Permission, Protection, and Potency have already been discussed. There are, however, a number of other qualities which facilitate quality interventions.

One of these variables is counselor patience. Counselors must have a great deal of patience. Part of this patience involves a sense of timing. Interventions must be made at appropriate moments in the counseling process; the pace should be neither too fast nor too slow. The client must have plenty of room in which to work. It should be apparent to the client that the counselor has time to spend with him. The counselor must show he cares, and this takes time.

The manner of the counselor must be confident; this engenders the aura of hope. Hearing the counselor say "Everything that is of discomfort to you can be treated" is very reassuring. In early stages when the relationship is not yet fully formed, the counselor must convey to the client that he will be taken care of. The counselor shows in many ways that he knows what he is doing.

For the client who is acutely suicidal, it is important that the counselor be willing to take charge. The counselor must be able to direct the client during the interview. The client might well feel helpless or out of control, and in these instances it is not helpful for the counselor to maintain a nondirective approach. Structure can be very calming. For clients who are highly lethal, the counselor must be willing to take steps to gain control of weapons or stockpiles of medicines. Family members or friends might have to be immediately notified to help protect the client from himself. Times of crisis are not times to be timid or indecisive.

Even at times of high risk where the counselor assumes a great deal of control, the client must be involved to the greatest degree possible in the development and implementation of plans. Cooperation between all parties is essential. Trust between those involved in the treatment process is also essential. Levels of trust grow as the relationship matures. Both parties come closer together during the process of counseling. The client's trust increases as he sees that the counselor struggles to understand and help. The counselor's trust in the client increases as he sees the client come to self-understanding and make changes in his life. The sought-after goal is to have the client be more prepared to handle his own affairs. To arrive at this point, the counselor as well as the client must be willing to trust each other and to let go of the relationship.

In addition to the positive variables of the counselor, there are certain negative aspects that must be considered.

At any stage of the counseling process there are a number of possible pitfalls for the counselor. Pretzell (1972) has outlined three primary problem areas. The counselor might over-react; in emergency situations it is easy to become panicked and feel overanxious. Use your common sense and remain calm. Under-reaction is a second possibility; emergencies do occur and they are stressful. Be in touch with your feelings and those of your client and act when action is required. Lastly, inappropriate action is possible. Keep the immediate situation in perspective with the client's history; do not miss the point of the critical incident. Make certain that you really hear the message of the client and act accordingly.

VARIABLES IN THE COUNSELING PROCESS

As with the client and the counselor, there are certain aspects of the counseling process that are unique in working with the suicidal. We will discuss some of the more important issues.

A Regular Client in Suicidal Crisis

At times, a client will be well along in a course of therapy before the issue of suicide surfaces, or some crisis might arise to which the client reacts with suicidal thoughts. In these situations it is up to the counselor to decide upon a treatment direction. The conservative approach would be to work at clarifying the death as an option issue and arriving at a no-kill contract as quickly as possible. Other therapy issues are temporarily put aside until some resolution about the immediate crisis and the issue of suicide is reached. In these instances the activity level of the therapist should increase dramatically because life is at stake.

Some therapists believe that such issues are only attempts at getting attention, and they might ignore or pay only slight attention to the suicidal material. This style of treatment might well result in fewer manipulative clients, but a higher number of dead ones. The conservative approach might result in a higher number of manipulative clients, but at least they would be alive.

Scheduling Sessions

In times of crisis the scheduling of counseling sessions can be varied. For many clients, the once a week session is not enough. It might be that one regular working session could be scheduled along with several supportive sessions of fifteen or so minutes each during the course of a week. The therapist should also make some sort of emergency arrangement with the client for night or weekend contact.

Getting Essential Information

The art of asking questions is very valuable to the counselor. For the new client, the counselor must not only have basic facts, but developmental information as well.

How did you decide to come for counseling today?
What has been happening to you lately?
What is happening now that is similar to what was happening to you before?
When did you begin to feel worse?
Have you felt this way before?
What is new in your life situation?
Who has been involved with you lately?

The above questions can provide a great deal of data in a relatively short time. Critical information about what has led up to the crisis period and how this might fit into a pattern helps in making the appropriate interventions.

There is also a great need to get concrete data from the suicidal client. In some instances, this can be very difficult to acquire. From the beginning the counselor must know such basic things as name, address, phone number, and friends to reach in case of emergency. It is also helpful to have an accurate physical description on file; even the make, model, description, and license number of the client's car is valuable. It may even be wise to keep a card with this information at the counselor's home. In time of acute crisis when the client might be actively suicidal, police would find this information invaluable.

Continuity of Treatment

Treatment of suicidal clients evolves through several stages and frequently involves more than one therapist. Coordination of the treatment in order that continuity be maintained is essential. In many instances the suicidal client is first seen in a state of crisis at some emergency facility. At this time the immediate self-destructive situation is remediated. The client is assisted in making a stay alive contract, and the precipitating factors are considered. It is not unusual for some sort of brief or short-term therapy to be initiated and even completed during the first stage. The client frequently feels better as the self-destructive urges are reduced; consequently, it is very common for the client and the counselor to terminate counseling or a referral is made to another counselor for long-term counseling, but the new contact is not firmly established. For a high proportion of suicidal clients, therapy of more than a crisis nature is called for. It is essential that the first counselor encountering the suicidal client make sure that some sort of long-term contract be arranged. Even if the precipitating elements are taken care of, the client may still be existing with an adjustment mechanism that involves death as an option. For many clients the return to the usual environment is very stressful, and a return of suicidal urges is common. If there is no continuity of treatment between the crisis and the long term, the death threat can return to a high point.

SUMMARY

Making appropriate interventions in the suicidal process is a complicated matter; there are many variables to consider. The individual counselor, client, and the specifics of the situation must all be taken into account. If the counselor is willing to be Potent, given Permission, and provide Protection, the success of the counseling is improved.

REFERENCES

Pretzell, Paul W. *Understanding and Counseling the Suicidal Person.* Nashville, Abingdon, 1972.

SUGGESTED READINGS

Barnes, Graham (Ed.): *Transactional Analysis After Eric Berne.* New York,

Har-Row, 1977.

Bellak, Leopold and Small, Leonard: *Emergency Psychotherapy and Brief Psychotherapy.* New York, Grune, 1965.

Fisher, Sheila A.: *Suicide and Crisis Intervention: Survey and Guide to Services.* New York, Springer Pub, 1973.

Frederick, Calvin J. and Resnik, H. L. P.: How suicidal behavior is learned. *Am J Psychother, 25*:37-55, 1971.

Grollman, Earl A.: *Suicide Prevention, Intervention, Postvention.* Boston, Beacon Pr, 1971.

Leonard, Calista V.: *Understanding and Preventing Suicide.* Springfield, Thomas, 1967.

Mendel, Werner M.: *Schizophrenia, The Experience and Its Treatment.* San Francisco, Jossey-Bass, 1976.

Moss, Leonard M. and Hamilton, Donald M.: The psychotherapy of the suicidal patient. *Am J Psychiatry, 112*:814-820, 1956.

Shelton, John L. and Ackerman, J. Mark: *Homework in Counseling and Psychotherapy.* Springfield, Thomas, 1976.

Shorr, Joseph E.: *Psycho-Imagination Therapy.* New York, Intercontinental Medical, 1972.

Sinnett, E. Robert: *Crisis Services for Campus and Community: A Handbook for the volunteer.* Springfield, Thomas, 1976.

Stone, Alan A.: Suicide precipitated by psychotherapy: a clinical contribution. *Am J Psychother, 25*:18-26, 1971.

Wolpe, Joseph: *The Practice of Behavior Therapy,* 2nd ed. New York, Pergamon, 1973.

Woollams, Stanley, Brown, Michael, and Huige, Kristyn: What transactional analysts want their clients to know. In Graham, Barnes (Ed.): *Transactional Analysis After Eric Berne: Teachings and Practices of Three TA Schools.* New York, Har-Row, 1977.

Chapter 5

CONTRACTS TO STAY ALIVE
AND GET WELL

CONTRACTS as a part of the therapeutic process have been used in a variety of settings. Over the years practitioners from the fields of social work, family therapy, group work, and behavior therapy, to mention but a few, have included contracts in the therapy process. Maluccio and Marlow (1974) have identified several critical characteristics of the contract.

Mutual agreement between the client and counselor is the first. The major participants in the process must have a sense of mutuality regarding the goals, roles, and tasks. This mutuality determines the direction, quality, and content of the counseling. As both parties deliberately map out directions, it becomes easier to work together and more difficult to clash because of opposing perspectives.

A second characteristic is differential participation. Both the counselor and client have different functions and responsibilities in the counseling process. The client by coming for assistance has set the stage to continue to be an active, self-governing individual and not to maintain a passive stance. As the contractual process unfolds, the client will make specific and general commitments to himself and to others. Agreements to engage in certain types of behaviors will be made. As the client carries out these commitments, feelings of achievement and competence usually develop. The counselor also agrees to provide certain functions. Most often these involve an agreement to treat the client for a given period of time, and to provide a certain type of support and protection while the client progresses through stages of change. The counselor agrees to serve as a guide during this period of change, with the implicit goal of reducing the amount of guidance as the client becomes more able to provide self-direction.

Reciprocal accountability is a third characteristic of the contract. From the beginning, both counselor and client have responsibilities to each other, such as keeping scheduled appointments, paying bills, following treatment suggestions, or being available in emergencies. As the contract evolves and develops, both individuals must work to be responsive to each other. The counselor is also accountable to his profession.

Explicitness is the final characteristic of the contract. In order to succeed, the statement of the contract must be very simple. Some therapists go so far as saying that if a contract cannot be stated in language understandable by a fourth grade student, it is probably not going to be carried out. The contract should be stated in clear, open, and specific terms. Both parties must know the point from which they are starting, where they intend to go, and how they are going to get there.

Application of the contractual process with suicidal clients is possible in two ways. First, the counselor is concerned with establishing conditions to insure that the client agrees to stay alive. At the same time, other contracts are developed which are aimed at the client getting well and getting on with life.

Contracts to Stay Alive

The suicidal client is a very complex individual. One facet is composed of a strong internal force that is extremely destructive, and another facet of the individual contains a powerful life-sustaining force. Counselors must be prepared to work with both aspects of the client as the contractual process evolves.

From the beginning of the counseling process, the therapist must gain a clear perspective of the total individual. The strength of the destructive force must be quickly and accurately assessed (see Chapter 3). All of the skills of the counselor must be employed so that the client knows he is understood in as many of his complexities as possible.

As soon as the self-destructive force becomes apparent, the counselor must begin to negotiate with the client so that an agreement can be made that the client will not kill himself.

This issue is discussed with the positive internal forces of the client since these are the aspects of his personality which have kept him alive up to this point. As much as possible, the negative or destructive forces are ignored during the formulation of the contract to stay alive. Development of a contract is similar to the process of establishing an intention or setting a goal.

The ideal contract is the client agreeing to the statement, "I will not kill myself accidently or on purpose, no matter what." This agreement can even be written out and signed by both parties. It is explained to the client that the primary thrust of the contract is that he is making an agreement with himself to stay alive. The secondary person involved in the contract is the therapist. Even though the counselor may be making the initial contract proposal, both parties through mutual consent are involved in its final construction and acceptance.

One more facet of the contract to live is its public nature. Our culture seems to have instilled in many individuals a code of honor focused on the importance of the act of giving someone your word. Consequently, when a client agrees to do something, most often he will honor that contract. If the contract is made in a group counseling setting, there appears to be even more importance placed upon it. The public nature, especially in a setting of caring peers, is a source of strong pressure to comply.

Specificity of the contract has a great deal of importance. The exact nature of what is to be done or not done must be outlined in clear, simple language. It is at this point where the simple language of the fourth grade student becomes applicable. For example, a statement like "I will not do away with myself" should be changed to "I will not kill myself." In a similar vein the statement "I will not kill myself without calling you first" is changed to "I will not kill myself without talking with you first." A client might call you and find the phone busy or not be able to speak with you directly. The specific agreement is to *talk* with you.

It is not uncommon for a suicidal client to have confused thinking; he may have a number of conflicting thoughts which may be very confusing and difficult to assimilate. An example would be his ambivalence about death; one minute he wants to kill himself while the next minute he wants to remain alive. The mechanical process of developing a clear contract can be very helpful in getting a client to slow down his thought process and think clearly. The counselor works at assisting him in putting his thoughts into words. As the client speaks about his thoughts, the usual result is for the individual to feel less confused, because in order to articulate them, he has had to organize them so they are clear to the listener. Therefore, it also becomes more concrete to the client.

It is not unusual for a client to be unwilling to give up death as an option for any extended period of time. In this situation, the counselor attempts to negotiate a contract for as long a period of time as possible. This might be a stay alive contract for as long as the client is in therapy, or it could be stated that "I will not kill myself during this next month." The shortest period of time that is acceptable is "I will not kill myself without talking with you first." Other variations that are acceptable in order to gain time to work with the client could include "I won't kill myself until next week" or "I won't kill myself until next spring." The counselor attempts to negotiate the longest time possible for the no-kill contract. Further, once the time approaches towards the expiration of the contract, the counselor negotiates a new one. All of this is predicated on the belief that over time most suicidal crises will resolve themselves; of course, counseling assists in the resolution.

Establishing the contract so the client will believe in it and have a firm commitment to upholding it is a life or death undertaking. The nature of the wording is especially crucial. Major points must be established, but the total message must not be so overwhelming that the client has only a slight chance of following through. Negotiation and contingency planning become essential. For the client who is unwilling to immediately give up life-threatening behavior, a negotiated contract might be for him to agree to show up, unhurt, at the next scheduled appointment. Another example would be for a client to agree to go immediately to a hospital emergency room if the destructive impulses begin to dangerously increase.

Reinforcement of success is an integral part of treatment. From the very beginning, the counselor must let the client know that his life-saving efforts are being noticed and appreciated. Statements by the counselor such as "I'm happy to see you, since I know how hard it is for you to come" or "I'm glad you kept your appointment today" are very important to the client.

A continuing theme in the use of contracts is the active involvement of the client. There must not be any doubt that the client has responsibility for his actions and has ultimate control of his behavior. While the therapist certainly has a great deal of impact, the client must clearly see the reality limits of the therapist. The therapist is not in a position to meet all of the needs of the client. To demonstrate this fact, the therapist might say "I am willing to work with you to the best of my ability, but I cannot treat you if you are dead." The therapist can go on to say "I need to know that you are willing to commit yourself to staying alive." For the client who has been in therapy for a time and already has a relationship established, the counselor could say, "If you kill yourself, I will be sad for a little while, but my life will go on." All of this keeps forcing the client to realize that he has ultimate responsibility for his own life.

Contracts Against Probable
Nonlethal Physical Harm

Many clients have a history of physically hurting themselves. This is extremely dangerous because of the possibility of death by accident. If you determine during the diagnostic assessment that a particular client has a history of instances of self-inflicted minor physical harm, action must be taken to terminate this behavior. An example would be wrist cutting, which the counselor detected by noting a number of scars on the wrists. Another example would be "accidently" taking too many pills while under the influence of alcohol, especially if this happened more than once. The contract in this instance might be, "I will not accidently or on purpose injure my body in any fashion, no matter what." Another modification would be, "I will take my medicine only according to instructions." The counselor must be creative and assist the client to develop a contract with special wording which meets the unique needs of the client.

Broken Contracts

A contract is usually thought of and explained as a commitment and not a promise. For some individuals, the term promise is a weaker form than the term commitment; these are the individuals who usually have a history of breaking promises. It is not a good counseling strategy to discuss with a client the idea of the contract being broken. It is a stronger, more positive position for the counselor to leave the client with the idea that there is no doubt that the contract will be honored in its entirety. However, it is important for the counselor to have thought through a course of action in the event that a client attempts to kill himself but does not succeed. We also do not encourage counselors to ever threaten a client with the idea that they will not be seen in therapy if they make any future life-threatening gestures.

In the event that a client does make a suicide attempt, the counselor must deal with the situation. From a treatment point of view, the episode would be debriefed in order to determine what was happening or not happening that led the client to resort to an attempt at self-destruction. The future stay-alive contract would be renegotiated with this new data in mind.

Refusal to Contract to Stay Alive

It is not unusual for a suicidal client to refuse to agree to a stay-alive contract. Clients can be very resistent, unwilling, or in their eyes unable to give up death as an option. For them, at that moment, they see no reason for life to continue. The future orientation of the stay-alive contract has no impactful meaning; consequently, they will not agree to it. From the client's eyes the future is of little importance or its negative case is so great that any positive features are over-shadowed.

In these instances the counselor has several options. If the client is so dangerous to himself that the counselor does not believe he will keep alive until the next appointment, then involuntary hospitalization is indicated. The counselor must take responsible action to guarantee the client's physical safety. Another option is open if the client is dangerous but not to such a lethal extent. At this point clinical judgment is really put to the test. It is at this juncture that the counselor begins to move away from the direct push for the establishment of a stay-alive contract which actively requires the client to put aside death as an option. Instead the counselor begins to work with the client toward getting a commitment which has a future orientation, no matter how slight. Examples of this are "I will not kill myself until after I talk with you again" or "I will show up at our next scheduled appointment without hurting myself" or "In the event that I feel so self-destructive before our next appointment, I will go to the hospital emergency room." Agreements of this type require that the client be taught how to present himself to the emergency room personnel in such a way that he will be taken seriously. In each of these examples the primary goal is to have the client agree to stay alive for a specific unit of time. As the client continues to stay alive, the possibilities increase that he will be able to work through the crisis.

Diagnostic Elements in Contract Negotiation

During the negotiation of the stay-alive contract, a great deal of information that can be used in further treatment strategies may surface. the client will often let the counselor know some of the primary obstacles in his life during this time. Such client comments as "I won't kill myself unless I am drunk" or "if my wife stops running around" or "until my mother dies" provide bridges to treatment of important issues. The counselor now knows more about which are the specific troubling issues in the client's life. At a later stage of treatment, these clues can be used by the counselor to initiate topics of discussion with the client.

Contracts Are Not Guarantees

After the development and acceptance of a stay-alive contract, the client as well as the counselor may feel a sense of relief. A major therapeutic step has been taken; to a great extent, the immediate pressure of the threat of death has been removed. For the client, the accomplishment of making a very important decision can start to bring about a stronger sense of personal competence and achievement. A new attitude of hope has been instilled by the mere fact that the degree of ambivalence has been reduced.

However, there is no magic quality in the commitment to a contract. Clients will continue to have ups and downs in their adjustment processes. As therapy progresses, new insights, new behaviors, and new awarenesses can well bring the client back to the brink of self-destruction. It is not unusual for clients to slip back into a previous level of depression after a time in therapy. The client's thoughts focus on the disappointment regarding not yet being completely well. Inner thoughts may be "I must really be hopeless; I have been in therapy three months and I still feel depressed." Suddenly death again becomes an immediate option.

It is essential that the counselor keep a sharp eye on the ups and downs of the client. For some, just the logical explanation that it takes time to get well and that there will be ups and downs will be enough. As the signs of increasing depression appear, the counselor must reaffirm the stay-alive contract. The emergency treatment contingencies must be reexplained and reinstituted when needed. Counselors must not become over-confident or complacent just because a client has, at one time, agreed to a stay-alive contract.

Contracts Used in the Getting
Well Treatment Phase

Contracts are very effective during all phases of treatment. As change takes place during the course of treatment, new contracts are negotiated to continue the change process. It becomes clearer to both the counselor and the client what the direction and purpose of counseling will be. Ambiguity is reduced, and this is the factor which many clients find comforting.

It is possible to have a number of contracts in effect at a given time. A client might be working at improving relationships with individuals at home as well as at work. In addition the client could be working at learning how to have more fun in life. The specifics of implementation of each contract must be individualized.

Part of every contract includes a statement of how both the client and counselor will know when the contract has been accomplished. This enables a clear evaluation of progress; consequently, total growth and change in therapy could be accelerated since less time would be wasted going over and over old material. It becomes easier to move on to new areas which need work.

REFERENCES

Maluccio, Anthony N. and Marlow, Wilma D.: The case for the contract. *Soc Work, 19(1)*:28-36, 1974.

Chapter 6

THE LIFE LINE

SELF-DESTRUCTIVE individuals have a tenuous hold on life. Their physical and emotional contacts with significant others, people in general, and professional helpers are neither firm nor frequent. It may even be difficult for them to carry on day-to-day life-sustaining activities such as eating, sleeping, or exercise. Consequently, an important counseling goal is the identification and implementation of life-sustaining activities. Together, the counselor and the client work to develop and maintain a number of contacts which will assist the client in performing these activities and to keep a grasp on life.

A client's life line is a composite of the counselor, friends, family, other agencies, activities, and instructions. The purpose of the life line is to offer the client someone or something to hold on to in the face of high level suicidal impulses.

PROFESSIONAL CONTACTS

Due to the commonness of withdrawal and isolation as a symptom of suicidal behavior, the counselor frequently becomes the primary human contact. Clients have often cut themselves off from friends and family. This is accomplished either figuratively or literally. A client might well have moved away from the family home or may have chosen to not associate with family or friends. The client may still be in physical contact with these individuals but for any number of reasons does not see them as emotional supports.

From the very first counseling contact, no matter how it is initiated, the counselor becomes a primary source of this life-sustaining support. A client may be first seen after an unsuccessful suicide attempt or when the individual decides to voluntarily discuss with a professional his suicidal thoughts and urges. The importance of this supportive contact usually increases as the counselor and client spend more time together. In initial counseling stages, the client believes that he is very weak and vulnerable, and the protection and nurturance provided by the counselor is very important.

As a main link in the life line, the counselor must plan with the client, so that maximum utilization and minimum abuse can be derived from the counseling process. Face-to-face contact during the counseling session is very important. In the time of crisis, the frequency of these contacts probably needs to be more than once a week. The counselor should also make plans with the client for contacts in the event of an emergency. This can be by phone or face-to-face during the evenings or on weekends. We believe it is essential for the counselor to be available to clients on an emergency basis. In the event that the counselor is not available, the client must know how to make contact with other sources of professional and nonprofessional support. Step-by-step contingency plans should be developed in order that the client is very clear as to how other helpers can be contacted. In the event the counselor is not available, the client might call whoever is the backup night or weekend counselor, or lacking this, there may be a crisis phone service that could be contacted. If the client believes that his suicidal urges are beyond his control, then the local hospital emergency room or the police department are sources of twenty-four-hour assistance. It is essential that the client be taught how to use these services. Realizing that hospitals are frequently overrun by hysterical individuals, the client must know how to present himself to the emergency room staff to let them know very directly the extent of his turmoil. If the police are called, the client must know that he certainly cannot meet them at the door carrying a weapon of any sort. He also must realize that if the police have to transport him, he can expect to be handcuffed. Careful education of the client will make it easier for him to constructively use the services of other professionals in the event of a crisis.

It is not unusual for suicidal clients to be treated by a number of professionals. A family physician might refer a client to a psychiatrist, or a psychologist might have a psychiatrist provide medication. The client may be in individual counseling with one counselor and in group counseling with another. The client may be in a day treatment facility in which any number of staff will be playing significant therapeutic roles. In situations such as these, it is important that continuity of care be maintained. All of the individuals providing counseling and consequently being part of the life line must be in close communication with each other. An agreed-upon treatment plan must be in operation and each individual must know his place in that plan. Any exception or emergency must be communicated as soon as possible to everyone involved with the case.

SIGNIFICANT OTHERS

Members of the client's immediate family can be a source of support during times of crisis as well as during the long-term counseling process. With the help of the counselor, the client can think through existing familial relationships and determine the existing strengths and weaknesses. Then strategies can be outlined by which the client can go on to maximize the strong relationships and shore up the weak ones. As the dynamics of the family system are discussed, the client becomes aware of which family members may be productively contacted and which need to be avoided under certain circumstances. It is not unusual that the counselor might have to prescribe to the client that he not contact certain family members. The client must quickly learn to evaluate his life space and be able to keep away from danger zones with respect to family.

Either the client or the counselor may initiate contact with friends or family in order to alert them to the critical nature of the client's distress or to actively seek their cooperation in the treatment plan. The counselor may decide that he should be the initiator, if the client is too confused or depressed to care for himself. A face-to-face interview would usually be the ideal, but a phone conversation is often all that is possible.

Family members at various times may be brought into the counseling process. For some clients, family therapy on a regular basis might be one part of the treatment plan. For others, education of the family members as to the seriousness of the suicidal position might be called for. Family members need to know exactly how they can be of help. Especially in times of life-threatening behavior, the counselor needs to be an active intervening force in the family system. The various members need to be told what to do and not do. It is not unusual for the family to be afraid to act responsibly around the identified client. They may think that they will set him off and precipitate another suicidal act, or in the other extreme, the family members might completely overlook the client's cries for help. In either case, an active educational stance with the client's family can be very helpful to the counseling process.

In order for family members to become effective links in the life line, they must have an awareness of their own reactions and position in the suicidal system. Since suicide can be a very threatening subject for discussion, it is not unusual for families to have developed various means of blocking their perceptions of the client's suicidal behavior. This blocking may be to such an extent that they actually have not heard any of the threatening verbalizations the client might have said. Other warning signs from the client such as withdrawal or depression may be ignored. Actual suicidal acts may be shrugged off as accidents. The family may become angry at the client because he is exposing them to situations that are very anxiety producing. The message may be "How could you do something like this when you know it hurts us?" Defense mechanisms of this type need to be pointed out to family members so they can learn to avoid possible problems in their interactions with the client.

Some family members will not talk directly about suicide with the client. They have the misconception that by talking about the subject, the chances of the client actually carrying through with the act increase. This is obviously not the case; talking is a safety valve, and the client at least has the concerned attention of a significant other. Others may feel that it is really none of their business. They may be apprehensive about invading the privacy of the client; instead many clients want their privacy invaded; they want to engage others in active conversation. Holding back from engaging the client is a way to ensure personal emotional safety. Family members often do not want to get too involved; they might fear the responsibility of being an active lifesaver. Education can play a significant part in helping these individuals understand that, for most potentially suicidal people, immediate emergency assistance is desired and is not necessarily a life-long commitment of support. These and other myths about the suicidal process need to be discussed openly with the involved family members. As their personal comfort increases, they will more likely become stronger resources in the client's life line.

Friends are another important link in the life line. Present and former friends and acquaintances can be integrated into the process of counseling. People contacts are essential to nurture the client from his position of isolation. Roommates can be involved in the life struggle. They need to be aware of what is going on with the client and how they might be of assistance. For example, at a time of suicidal threat, friends might be enlisted to stay with the client until he feels more in control of his impulses. Careful work with the client will enable him to reach out to close personal contacts and thereby increase the number of people who are potential sources of support.

Individuals such as classroom teachers and ministers also need to be included in the client's life line. For many clients these people can be a great source of support. Frequently, teachers and ministers are held in high esteem and there can be a great deal of trust placed on them. Consequently, they need to be informed of the client's situation and how they might be of assistance.

All of the family and friends of the client need to be informed of the possible phases of treatment. In the beginning phases of treatment, the counselor will most likely be the one to contact significant others. In later phases, the client should be actively involved in this process to the extent that he is able. These significant others need to have some global view of what the client is experiencing and what behaviors might be exhibited. In the event that the suicidal behavior is reactivated and intensified, they will need to be helped through this period of discouragement. It is not unusual for family members to begin to feel hostile and even display subtle forms of rejection if the client does not get well fast enough. Significant others also need to find the balance between being too gentle with the client and having too high expectations. The client will need support and nurturance, but he will also need an opportunity to develop independence and take increasing responsibilty. It is up to the counselor to act as a consultant to all of the involved members of the client's sytem; in this manner all of the links in the life line stand an opportunity to remain strong and intact.

For all significant others, the primary source of contact is the client. The counselor can work with the client so he feels comfortable about informing others of his emotional situation. The process of learning that it is all right to ask for help and discovering that many will respond constructively to requests can be very beneficial to the client. There are many implications to this, one being that the client is not alone and others will respond to him.

Depending upon the nature of the crisis and the counselor's personal ethical stance, it might be that the counselor has to be the primary source of contact with the pool of significant others. In the beginning it might be a lifesaving step for the counselor to begin to inform friends and family of the client's situation. This could be done even without the client's permission (see Chapter 9). In emergencies, we believe the boundaries of confidentiality may be bent. For some clients it is too threatening, in early stages of counseling, to talk directly with their sources of support. In these instances the counselor might be the one to intervene in his behalf. This can be accomplished with the client's permission. Certainly, as time goes by, it is necessary for the client to assume more and more of this responsibility.

LIFE SUPPORT ACTIVITIES FOR THE CLIENT

While the life line is anchored by the counselor, the client must, as soon as possible, be completely responsible for his life. This requires that a great deal of homework or behavioral practice be carried on outside of the counseling session. Shelton and Ackerman (1974) believe that it is very important that this practice be systematically integrated into the treatment plan.

A beginning task is for the client to identify situations which he reacts to by moving closer to self-destruction. Following this is to identify those situations to which he reacts by moving further away from suicidal thoughts and behavior. The formulation of these two lists can be very helpful in moving the client to look at how he can regulate his own life. He is being taught to be prepared for the bad times as well as the good. It can be reassuring to learn that he is not helpless and there are things he can do to protect himself.

Using questions is one way to assist the client to identify people and activities which are sources of positive support.

What is dear to you?

What has value in your life?

What needs to happen so that life will become worth living for you?

Who will cry and be sad when you die?

Questions such as these provide a stimulus for insightful thinking. As the client provides answers to these questions, he is setting the stage for future action steps. He is gaining a clearer picture of whom he might contact or what he might do, so that he will begin to feel better. Some clients might respond to the questions by saying that nothing is dear to them or that no one cares for them. The counselor can again use questions by asking, "How can you go about finding people who care?" or "What can you do to put value to your life?" The thrust is always toward getting the client to recognize that he has responsibility for, and control over, what happens in his life. He is in a position to take steps to keep a grasp on life.

For the individual who has low impulse control and needs firm guidance, a daily schedule can be helpful. Together the counselor and the client will outline hour by hour and day by day exactly what the client will be doing. Specific tasks will be either assigned by the counselor or developed by the client. This structure is very reassuring to the confused and frightened client. Activity can lift despair and give purpose to existence. For some individuals, it is helpful to carry their lists with them so in the event of panic they can take out their list and look at it and have something concrete to which to react.

The content of the daily schedule will vary from client to client. It might include making phone calls to or visiting one or two significant others each day. This type of homework is aimed at reintegrating the client with the people in his life. Simple but basic life-sustaining activities could also be included: getting out of bed, cooking and eating meals, or taking a bath. For some regressed individuals, a friend might be recruited to monitor such activities. For the more integrated client, items involving work or school may be outlined. The planned schedule assists the client to keep a sense of perspective over his life and avoids the chance of being overwhelmed.

A basic element of the use of homework and activity schedules is the factor of being future-oriented. A pattern among the suicidal is to be past-oriented and to believe that the future holds nothing for them. Consequently, throughout counseling an effort is made to have the client work in the present and plan and look toward the future in a positive manner. It becomes increasingly difficult for the client to consider suicide if his life is busy and productive and future-oriented.

REFERENCES

Shelton, John L. and Ackerman, J. Mark: *Homework in Counseling and Psychotherapy.* Springfield, Thomas, 1974.

SUGGESTED READINGS

Cain, Albert C.: *Survivors of Suicide.* Springfield, Thomas, 1972.

Chapter 7

THE THERAPIST'S PERSONAL
REACTION TO SUICIDE

THE counselor in dealing with the suicidal client assumes a different role than in working with other types of clients. The counselor is more active, directive, and consequently becomes more "responsible" for the direction of the counseling process. Not only does the counselor take more responsibility for direction, but further, he tolerates client dependence and actually encourages it. As Light (1973) states, "Specifically, the therapist initially supports and controls the patient's life. Regaining hope, the patient improves markedly, but in a way highly dependent on the therapist. Sometimes the therapist does not recognize how strong this dependency is. The therapist backs away, emphasizes the provocative and childish nature of the patient's dependence and rejects the patient." This is the quandry that is imperative for the counselor to avoid. Somehow, the counselor must effectively encourage dependence, but on the other hand be conscious of it and take steps to wean the client away from dependence. This may be accomplished by the introduction of significant others in the client's life into the therapeutic process, as mentioned in Chapter 6. However, what of the counselor's feelings during this process?

It is important that the counselor share his concerns about the potential life-threatening behavior of his client with the significant others of the client. This allows a "distribution" of treatment responsibility, although the counselor remains the coordinator of this treatment team. It can also afford the counselor some peace of mind, in that others will also be involved in the life-sustaining supports of the client. Therefore, the counselor has a treatment network. In the event matters become worse for the client, the counselor has the assurance that these others can act to support the client, as well as get in touch with the counselor. The counselor may then employ whatever crisis intervention techniques would be appropriate for the situation.

For many counselors, the tragic mistake is in making the subtle shift of being responsible for the treatment of the client to being responsible for the life of the client. These feelings can generate profound anxiety in the counselor, and as Basescu (1965) points out, it is precisely the therapist's anxiety about suicide that reduces his effectiveness in working with the client. How does the counselor keep his feelings of responsibility in perspective?

Litman (1968) states, "In my experience the most effective way for a therapist in any setting to deal with his anxiety over the possibility of a patient's committing suicide is to share it with one or more colleagues, by formal and informal consultations in a spirt of mutual support, repeated until the anxiety is dispelled." It is critical for the counselor to follow Litman's suggestion. If not, the counselor is left terribly alone with his feelings of total responsibility for the life of another. To the extent that the counselor is alone with these feelings is the extent to which they may become destructive to both the counselor and the client. This further allows these feelings to take on greater complexity. What, for the counselor, was once feelings of responsibility, fear, and anxiety, become feelings of anger, hostility, powerlessness, and incompetence. It is critical for the counselor to defuse these feelings in order that they do not mushroom and become a major obstacle to the counselor in working with the client.

Any counselor who has been in this situation readily recognizes what is being discussed. Counselors are trained as autonomously functioning professionals. Unfortunately, it is not common practice for counselors to seek the support of their peers for fear of embarrassment or perhaps of being perceived as incompetent. Further, as professionals, we tend to depersonalize our real feelings and to look at them through abstract constructs. We may believe that if we can label them, they become safe. In discussing our feelings with our colleagues, it is as important for us to be as open as we expect our clients to be. If we are afraid, it is important to ventilate this feeling in order that it not control us. And, if we are angry with the client, in spite of our efforts, he will not get better. If we feel put upon by the constant demands on our time made by the difficult suicidal client, these feelings then get in the way in dealing with the client.

The counselor, then, is encouraged to seek out the support of his professional peers to allow himself the opportunity to deal with his feelings openly and honestly. It further serves the purpose of allowing the counselor the opportunity of sharing case strategy, treatment objectives, etc., with his colleagues. By sharing his strategies before implementing them, the counselor is provided with the opportunity of testing his plans with a respected colleague.

Another point to consider, in the tragic event the client does take his own life, the counselor will have already established a working relationship with the professional peer, who may then assist the counselor in his personal reaction to the loss of the life of his client.

Further, the counselor, in having discussed the case and the treatment plans, has some assurances that his particular treatment with the deceased client was professionally reasonable although sorrowfully unsuccessful. This may be an important protection for the counselor in the event his treatment is called into question in the process of any legal recourse taken by relatives of the deceased.

OTHER FACTORS TO CONSIDER

It is apparent by now that large amounts of time and energy may be required of the counselor in treating the suicidal client. Both time and energy are finite; the counselor only has so much to go around. Consequently, it is strongly suggested that the counselor limit the number of actively suicidal clients he deals with at any point in time. It is hard for us to conceive of any counselor being able to treat more than two or three active suicidal clients. If the counselor does not heed this advice, he will become exhausted and perhaps more important, because of his fatigue, his judgment may become impaired in dealing with his suicidal clients. Counselors must take care of themselves before they can be expected to treat others.

In the event of a completed suicide, the psychological autopsy may be a worthwhile endeavor. A psychological autopsy attempts to recreate those events prior to and including the suicidal act. It includes family, school, medical, and work history through reports of others. The psychological autopsy permits the counselor, and his colleagues, to come to better understand the complete gestalt of the deceased client. This may help the counselor learn from the case and apply that learning in dealing with future suicidal clients. It also allows the counselor the opportunity to put the case in "clinical" perspective which may help him resolve any feelings of personal and professional failure. Psychological autopsies also usually result in colleague support of the counselor, and if the counselor did everything in his power to prevent the loss, there will be resulting colleague sanction and approval of the counselor's behavior leading up to the death of his client.

This support and case review is also necessary in helping the counselor come to closure with the case. If closure is not forthcoming, the counselor may become "gun shy" in his willingness to see future clients who may be suicidal in nature.

REFERENCES

Basescu, Sabert: The threat of suicide in psychotherapy. *Am J Psychother, 19*:99-105, 1965.

Light, Donald W.: Treating suicide: the illusions of a professional movement. *Am Soc Service J, 25*:475-487, 1973.

Litman, Robert: Psychotherapist's orientations toward suicide. In Resnik, H.L.P. (Ed.): *Suicidal Behaviors: Diagnosis and Management.* Waltham, Ma, Little, 1968.

Chapter 8

THE USE OF THE
TELEPHONE IN TREATMENT

THE telephone is an important element in any counseling treatment plan. Its use allows for an infinite extension and expansion of the counselor's availability and skills. Careful use of the phone is a time-saver for both the client and the counselor. In this chapter we will discuss the use of the telephone as part of emergency and crisis intervention, and as an element in ongoing treatment.

EMERGENCY TREATMENT

For most counselors the telephone is used primarily in crisis situations. The client is communicating by the mere act of telephoning that he is experiencing a difficulty that he thinks needs immediate attention. In all probability the client is experiencing intense discomfort. He is most likely to be in a fearful panic state and having difficulty thinking in a rational manner. Feelings of helplessness and a fear of losing control are common. A primary goal for the client is to be rescued; he believes that he is not capable of dealing with his current situation by himself.

If it is the first contact the counselor has ever had with the client, the first goal is to establish some sort of relationship. It is at this point where such basic counseling skills as active listening, nonjudgmental responses, reflection of feeling, and paraphrasing are important. As the counselor assists the caller to talk about his situation, the beginnings of a helping relationship are developed. Some level of readiness is indicated by the fact that the client has chosen to call.

Using the phone as a means to help someone in crisis is somewhat different than talking with him face to face in the office. All of the skills that are used when the counselor is

86

interviewing a client in person are used when he is using the telephone. Active listening and assertive communication skills are essential. The counselor's task is to put together a great deal of information based on just the voice of the caller. Whispers, choked replies, crying, rise and fall of tone, hesitancies in replies, inflections, and expressions of doubt, to mention but a few, must be responded to in an active fashion. The client also has fewer cues to respond to; consequently, the counselor must be able to use his voice to convey a great deal of acceptance and understanding. The counselor can use changes in tone, inflection, and volume to show that he is working hard at understanding. He must be willing to ask questions and respond from intuition. Statements like "Do I hear tears in your voice?" can help the caller say more about what is being experienced. The counselor searches for more information by asking, "Do I hear doubt in your voice?" or "You sound frightened." For a counselor who is used to seeing as well as hearing a client, phone counseling can be very difficult.

All of the counselor's energies are aimed at building the relationship and sense of rapport. This can be done by showing the caller that the counselor is, indeed, paying attention and that he cares. Since head nodding will not do, the counselor must indicate his acceptance in a verbal manner. This involves direct communication that is conveyed by such statements as "I understand" or "I hear what you're saying." Also, by active questioning the counselor moves on to help the client clearly identify the problem, just exactly what is happening to the person and what is he reacting to. Resources available to the caller must be identified, assessed, and eventually mobilized. When a person is alone with just a phone as a link to the outside world, other individuals can be important sources of support. Finally the specific plan of action must be determined. The client must think and feel that there is some hope; that the effort to call was worth the expended energy.

Telephone work requires that the counselor be creative in the use of his voice. A sense of competence and calmness must be quickly conveyed. This can be done in many ways: speaking calmly, softly, being accepting and gentle, or being firm and rational are all examples.

The counselor must be ready to suggest and inform. Panic can arise from a lack of information; knowing facts can be reassuring. Keeping the caller talking is a major goal. If nothing else, the counselor is buying time. By talking, the client is slowing down his thinking and thereby gaining a better perspective. The rush of ideas becomes slower and easier to deal with. Positive action steps somehow seem to become more of a possibility.

It is important for the counselor to remember that he is not trying to solve all of the client's problems during this conversation. Solution to only the major reason for panic is the primary goal. If this is not possible, the objective becomes the assurance of the client that the obstacle can be dealt with in counseling. The details of the precipitating sequence can all be debriefed at a later date. It is not important to seek information that will not be helpful at the moment. The life line that is being thrown to him is not intended to keep him going forever, but to keep him alive long enough for him to take a more logical look at the immediate situation or to get him involved in counseling. Unfortunately, in some instances the counselor will not have another contact with the individual. The conversation is intended to slow down the client's rush toward death; happy endings are not guaranteed.

When the caller is in the midst of a suicidal crisis, it is essential for the counselor to find out as much basic information about the individual as possible. There is no certainty that the counselor will be able to provide all of the assistance necessary, so information must be obtained that will be helpful in getting the client appropriate help. It must be determined exactly who is calling, where they are calling from, and what is the phone number. Questions to elicit this information can be woven into the contents of the call, or the data can be asked for directly. If nothing else, an example of honesty and directness is being set for the client. If the client has done something to injure himself, the counselor should find out the method and the extent of the injury; for example, in the case of an overdose, one should ask what pills were taken, as well as approximately how many and when. It might even be appropriate to ask the client what he looks like and to describe what he is wearing. In the event that the police need to be called or an ambulance needs to be dispatched, all of this information is essential.

For the counselor who has developed a good professional reputation, it is not unusual to get a number of unsolicited crisis phone calls. Tuckman (1970) has enumerated a number of options that the counselor might initiate. Medical emergencies such as overdoses and slashed wrists should be referred to hospital emergency rooms. Emotional crises with high energy components such as deep depression with suicidal thoughts and low impulse control can be dealt with by establishing contact and hearing the person out. The caller needs to know that he is being taken seriously and that the counselor is willing to provide help. Either a face-to-face meeting or hospitalization might be required. Calls from relatives or friends describing the two previous situations can be handled by assisting the significant other to arrange for either voluntary or involuntary hospitalization. Significant others, seeking guidance, might also call about clients not in your immediate area. In these situations, the therapist can help by hearing the caller out and providing reassurance as well as specific steps as to how to locate sources of support which are closer geographically to the identified client.

It is a common occurrence to get calls from seriously disturbed individuals who are not specifically suicidal and with a concern that is not immediate. These individuals can be listened to, reassured, and referred for a face-to-face contact with an appropriate agency.

The client whose regular counselor is unavailable or out of town may also be a caller. In these instances it is best to hear the person out, reassure, and provide the immediate assistance that is needed. The caller must be encouraged to contact the regular counselor as soon as possible. The counselor might receive repeated calls from someone who does not seem to be in any physical danger or real emotional crisis. These people need to be encouraged to set a face-to-face appointment with an appropriate agency as soon as possible. It is likely that the caller could suffer from some sort of hysterical disorder, and crisis intervention is not doing him any long-term good.

In each of these instances the counselor attempts to establish rapport, assess the lethality, identify the problem, determine the resources, and establish a plan. A major dependence is placed upon the caller to find, at the end of the call, a source of more long-term assistance. The counselor must be prepared to have the call end with many loose ends not yet accounted for.

THE REGULAR CLIENT

For the established client who is going through a situational life crisis where death becomes an immediate and pressing option, the counselor can give permission to call if there is a need. There are many ways in which to structure this permission. Saying "I am listed in the phone book and I want you to feel free to look up my number and call if you are in crisis" is much different from just handing a client a slip of paper with your name and number on it and explaining "It is OK to call if the need is great." The first option has undertones that suggest that the client has strength to make it without calling; the second option encourages more dependence. Another way to give permission, promote independence, and provide a boost of confidence is to say "It is perfectly all right to call me, but I don't think you will need to do that." It is important for the counselor to set limits when permission is given to call. The client must be told that he will not always be available when he calls. This shows the client that he cannot expect to get everything he needs from his counselor. He must be prepared to make use of the life line that has been worked out together.

Clients must also be told that the therapist is willing to spend time with them on the phone, but that there are limits. The counselor might say "If I have five minutes, I will gladly talk with you, but then I will have to go." It is a good idea to be direct and honest with the client and to let him know of the time limits. For personal survival and comfort the counselor must be able to structure a call so that it does not go on and on.

It is essential to focus on the critical issues, find alternatives, and set a course of action. Only so much material can be adequately discussed on the phone and the client must realize this; the counselor has to tell the caller that a given topic will have to wait until the next session. Both parties must accept responsibility for finding the primary issues and setting priorities for discussion.

In each instance, a portion of the next regular counseling session must be used to debrief the previous crisis call. This helps show the client that he is responsible for his actions. It is also a way in which the client can learn new skills for dealing with emergencies. The educational aspects of counseling must always be kept in view. There is always a danger that responding to a crisis call can set a dangerous precedent; for the client, finding someone to rescue him can easily become a game. There is also a possibility that the counselor would be teaching clients to act helpless so they will get service.

GENERAL CONSIDERATIONS

For the unknown caller the phone has a number of distinct advantages. The caller is clearly placed in control and can remain anonymous if he chooses. The counselor is also anonymous and this sense of distance helps some people feel more at ease and able to talk freely. Self-esteem can be saved in the eyes of some individuals if they are talking to a stranger who cannot see them. The dim figure in a confessional is somewhat similar. For the person in crisis, this type of help seeking may be a way in which to help him keep up the facade that he really has no problems. He rationalizes his call by thinking that his situation of upset is only temporary. The telephone also offers a very immediate source of support. There is not a long waiting period; immediate contact with a helping person can often be established.

A primary goal of any counseling intervention is to impact the client in a positive manner. The crisis caller is a likely candidate for change because of the high degree of emotionality. It is at these times that clients are the most emotionally accessible. In noncrisis situations the defenses are frequently up, and it is more difficult to get the client to work from his emotional base. Consequently, while the risk is high and there is high danger, there is opportunity for the client to come to some emotional understandings that might otherwise not be achieved if it were not for the emergency. Given this fact the counselor could well press on certain issues if it seemed that there was a good chance for therapeutic gain.

Because of the potential for crisis calls, it is important that all counselors develop good habits in regard to returning phone calls. Due to the press of time, many counselors have different systems for returning calls. It is our belief that calls should be returned within the hour, and messages should not be allowed to accumulate. Secretaries should be trained so that they can detect the real emergency and pass the message on to the counselor immediately.

Secretaries and receptionists are the first line of defense in handling initial contacts with clients. For both cases of face-to-face as well as telephone contact, it is critical for a positive impression be made. Office personnel must be warm and responsive to clients. It is their sensitivity, intuition, common sense, education, and special training that works in combination so they can separate the routine client from the emergency. After they have assessed the nature of the call, they must be able to make a smooth referral to the appropriate staff member. For instance, in the event of a counselor being tied up they could say, "Mr. Jones is seeing a client now, but he will be able to call you at the hour."

Answering services also should be selected with care. Some services answer a call by saying the phone number, "This is 385-4141." Others will give your name, "Dr. Jones' answering service, may I help you?" We believe that the personal approach is best. The counselor must be confident that the service will be able to judge how best to refer emergency calls.

The telephone can be used to the client's advantage or disadvantage. It is an important counseling tool; consequently, all counselors should review the systems that are used in their counseling office.

REFERENCES

Tuckman, Jacob: Suicide and the suicide prevention center. In Wolf, Kurt: *Patterns of Self-Destruction.* Springfield, Thomas, 1970.

SUGGESTED READINGS

Delworth, Ursula, Rudrow, Edward H., and Taub, Janet (Ed.): *Crisis Center/Hotline: A Guidebook to Beginning and Operating.* Springfield, Thomas, 1972.

Fisher, Sheila A.: *Suicide and Crisis Intervention: Survey and Guide to Services.* New York, Springer Pub, 1973.

Lamb, Charles W.: Telephone therapy: some common errors and fallacies. *Voices, 5(4)*:42-46, 1970.

Lester, David and Brockopp, Gene W. (Eds.): *Crisis Intervention and Counseling by Telephone.* Springfield, Thomas, 1973.

Orten, James D.: A transactional approach to suicide prevention. *Clin Soc Work J, 2(1)*:42-46, 1974.

Sifneos, Peter E.: *Short-term Psychotherapy and Emotional Crisis.* Cambridge, Harvard U Pr, 1972.

Sinnett, E. Robert: *Crisis Services for Campus and Community: A Handbook for the Volunteer.* Springfield, Thomas, 1976.

Chapter 9

LEGAL AND ETHICAL CONSIDERATIONS FOR THE SUICIDAL CRISIS

Cᴏɴғɪᴅᴇɴᴛɪᴀʟɪᴛʏ is the ethical cornerstone of the mental health professions. It is the foundation upon which trust is built in the counseling relationship. However, each of the mental health professions recognize that confidentiality is not absolute (Group for the Advancement of Psychiatry Committee of Psychiatry and Law, 1966; APA, 1977; Levy, 1976; APGA, 1974). In each discipline the license to break confidentiality is contingent upon the client being a clear and imminent danger to himself or to others. This ethical code of the various mental health professions, however, is not to be confused with privileged communication.

Privileged communication is granted by statute, whereby a legislative body of the state accepts the particular mental health profession's contention that confidentiality is a necessary prerequisite for the protection of the client to openly engage in the therapeutic process. In only nine states do counselors have legislatively granted privileged communication.

There is also a great deal of variability from state to state with respect to the other mental health professions and privileged communication. Even in those states where privileged communication is granted to a given professional group, it only protects the client from the counselor testifying as to what transpired in a counseling session in a court of law. Privileged communication, however, has little to do with whether confidentiality is to be broken or not in any given situation. The exception to confidentiality lies with the counselor's judgment as to whether the client represents a "clear and imminent danger." The key here is counselor's judgment.

If the client is unwilling to enter into a stay-alive contract and is clearly and imminently suicidal, the counselor is obligated to break confidentiality. What is less clear, however, is when confidentiality is to be broken with whom does the counselor share his concern? The term "counselor" in the previous sentence is used generically.

The answer to the question varies, depending upon the mental health profession of the "counselor" and his particular profession's code of ethics. It is further complicated by the fact that most codes of ethics are formulated on such an abstract level that they merely provide general guides to actual behavior (Fox, 1959) and practitioners rarely understand how they apply in a given situation (Bersoff, 1975). To further cloud this issue, is the problem that ethics are developed for a profession, by a profession, in an abstract manner. It remains unclear as to what the courts' positions may be with respect to the various interpretations of codes of ethics.

TO WHOM DOES THE MENTAL HEALTH PROFESSIONAL BREAK CONFIDENTIALITY?

The Ethical Standards of Psychologists (1966) states in Principle 6a: "Information received in confidence is revealed only after most careful deliberation and when there is clear and imminent danger to an individual or to society, and then to appropriate professional workers or public authorities."

Notice the above statement makes no reference to family or friends. Therefore, one can interpret the above statement to mean a psychologist may only break confidentiality to a professional colleague or to law enforcement officials. This places the psychologist in an ethical dilemma in working with the suicidal client. Very often it is in the client's best interest to seek out the support of his family in trying to convince the client of the necessity of hospitalization. Without the family support a voluntary hospitalization may have to become an involuntary commitment to a state hospital. And this action further alienates the client from the counselor in that the counselor has taken "action against" his client.

Also, family support often is critical for the counselor once the client is in the hospital, in order that they may assist the counselor in assisting the client. In the event the psychologist had to initiate commitment procedures and was obligated not to contact the family prior to doing so (as would be required by the APA ethics statement), family support may be delayed since the primary concern of the family would be for the psychologist to justify to them why it was necessary for him to take such a drastic action as committing the client. Consequently, the family may resent the psychologist since the family had not been consulted before such action was taken.

The ethical position of the American Psychological Association precludes family involvement unless the psychologist has the client's consent. Yet many suicidal clients very much resist any suggestions by the counselor that the family be told of the client's condition. In spite of this, once the counselor has done so, the client is relieved. At last the significant others in his life know the extent of his anguish, which up until now he was unwilling or unable to share with those he most loves. Once the family is knowledgeable of the client's condition, they can become an integral aspect of the treatment. However, the ethical position of the APA makes it difficult for the psychologist to exercise a reasonable treatment act on his client's behalf.

This position has not been tested in the courts. A recent case decided by the California Supreme Court, known as *Tarasoff v. Regents of University of California** found a psychologist liable for not informing the family of an intended murder victim of the potential threat of his client. The client murdered the victim. It is important to point out, however, that the psychologist did follow the prescribed ethical procedure of the American Psychological Association in that the psychologist conferred with two other clinicians, followed by formal letter, requesting a commitment of the client to a mental health facility, and notified the police. The police subsequently released the client when the client agreed to stay away from the woman.

Although the analogous situation with respect of suicide has not been tested, is it not just as probable that a court could rule in the event of a successful suicide, even if the psychologist had notified the proper authorities, that the family of the potential

---

*Tarasoff v. Regents of University of California, 13 C.3d 177, 529 P.2d 553, 118 Cal. Rptr. 129 (1974).

victim (suicide) has the same right of warning as decided in the *Tarasoff* case? Again we have the situation where an ethical guideline has yet to be sanctioned by the courts.

Psychiatrists' guidelines for therapeutic "deviations" from confidentiality appear to be less confining to the practitioner. The Group for the Advancement of Psychiatry, Committee of Psychiatry and Law (1966) states, ". . . the psychiatrist, on occasion, may appear to deviate from the ethical position of confidentiality . . . situations arise in therapy which force the psychiatrist to deviate from his original commitment. However, all these deviations are governed by the same basic principle of the ultimate personal welfare of the patient. Psychiatrists, more often than their medical colleagues, have patients whose mental states change so that they may no longer act effectively and appropriately for themselves. Under these circumstances, the physician is obliged to make certain decisions in the best interest of his patients." This appears to give the psychiatrist the perogative to act within his best judgment as opposed to having the ethical statement so rigid as to preclude certain actions which the psychiatrist feels would be in the best interest of the client.

The ethical standards prescribed by the American Personnel and Guidance Association with respect to the limits of confidentiality state, "In the event that the counselee or client's condition is such as to require others to assume responsibility for him, or when there is clear and imminent danger to the counselee or client or to others, the member (counselor) is expected to report this fact to an appropriate responsible authority, and/or take such other emergency measures as the situation demands." This statement appears to give the counselor the flexibility to act responsibly in the acute suicidal crisis without the counselor having to worry about whether he is following strict "p's and q's" of procedures prescribed by an interpretation of an ethical position as is the case with the psychologist. Therefore, the counselor may initiate contact with those people or authorities that may be of the most benefit to the counselor and/or client in the suicidal crisis.

LEGAL IMPLICATIONS FOR THE COUNSELOR

At one time or another a counselor will be treating a suicidal client whose treatment demands exceed the skill available to the counselor. Of course, the counselor's first concern is in doing what is in the best interest of the client. However, another dynamic also emerges in this situation. The counselor wants to make sure what he does is "right" so that in the tragic event the client does kill himself the counselor's actions were beyond reproach. In other words the counselor must have some concern with protecting himself.

This is an unfortunate reality in today's professional world. We have all become suit and malpractice conscious. Perhaps, we allow these fears to take on too much weight. Bergum and Anderson (1975) state "No firm doctrinal footing has yet been established to draw a clear line as to what conceivably might be ruled malpractice in a counselor-counselee situation." They further state "No court decision specifically relates to the counselor and counselee . . ." This may or may not relieve our concerns, but hopefully it may help counselors keep in perspective the liability issue. It is further important to point out that malpractice suits are not based upon a counselor making a wrong decision or making a mistake, but rather it is based upon a counselor being grossly negligent in his actions. His actions would have to be inconsistent with current practice standards of his profession. Therefore, counselors, as all other professionals, have the right to make mistakes and these mistakes would not be viewed as negligence, providing the counselor's actions were reasonable and prudent in the light of the information the counselor had at hand.

Malpractice cases in counseling would typically fall under civil liability adjudications. "Civil liability, simply stated, means that one can be sued for not doing right, or for doing wrong to another. Judicial relief is generally in the form of damages awarded to the wronged party" (Bergum & Anderson, 1975). What then would be considered malpractice for the counselor in the dealing with a suicidal client?

The counselor is a professional with recognized skills. It is the utilization of these skills that the public has a right to demand. However, there are limits to any counselor's skills. The counselor has the obligation to society to only render services within these limits. If the client's problems are such that the services needed are greater than the skills that the counselor has available to him, the counselor has the responsibility to refer the client to an individual or agency that can provide the client with treatment resources indicated. The situation does not require the counselor to be responsible for "effecting a cure." If the counselor felt the client was experiencing problems that he himself was not trained to treat, he is obligated to refer the client to an appropriately trained expert such as a psychologist or psychiatrist (Bergum and Anderson, 1975). If the counselor did not refer, and the client killed himself, the counselor could be considered negligent in a court of law.

This is not to say that a counselor must refer every suicidal client to a psychologist or psychiatrist. This is where the issue becomes cloudy for the counselor, particularly if he is liability conscious. It is very probable that many counselors have excellent training and skills in working with suicidal clients. Ultimately, the counselor has to individually evaluate the client's service needs through the counselor's assessment of his own skills and experience. It is further important to point out that, although Bergum and Anderson (1975) suggest referring the client to a psychologist or psychiatrist, these professionals do not necessarily have any more specialized skill in working with the suicidal client than does the counselor who is referring the client.

Unfortunately, there are no easy answers to the difficult question as to when the counselor should refer his client to someone with more expertise in suicide intervention. The answer to the question, except in the situation where a suicide attempt is imminent, must lie in the counselor's assessment of his skills. It is urged that the counselor not make the decision just on the basis of protecting himself for fear of legal repercussions, particularly since a referral made too hastily can have a serious negative emotional impact on the client.

REFERENCES

American Psychological Association: *Ethical Standards for Psychologists,* 1977 Revision. Washington, DC, APA, 1977.

American Personnel and Guidance Association: *Ethical Standards.* Washington, DC, APGA, 1974.

Bergum, Thomas and Anderson, Scott: *The Counselor and the Law.* Washington, DC, APGA Press, 1975.

Bersoff, Donald N.: Professional ethics and legal responsibilities. On the horns of a dilemma. *J Sch Psychol, 13(4):*359-576, 1975.

Fox, Renee C.: *Experiment Perilous.* Glencoe, Ill, Free Pr, 1959.

Group for the Advancement of Psychiatry. Committee of Psychiatry and Law: *Confidentiality and Privileged Communication in the Practice of Psychiatry,* No. 45. New York, Group for the Advancement of Psychiatry, 1960.

Levy, Charles S.: *Social Work Ethics.* New York, Human Sci Pr, 1976.

Chapter 10

MEDICAL AND CHEMOTHERAPEUTIC INTERVENTIONS

THE decision as to whether to hospitalize a suicidal client is probably one of the most difficult decisions encountered by a counselor. Since the decision is so frought with feelings, it becomes even more important for the counselor to have realistic expectations as to what probably will and will not occur when his client is in the hospital. It is also critically important for the counselor to come to grips with the issues which will affect the decision as to whether to hospitalize or not.

WHEN IS HOSPITALIZATION NECESSARY?

In earlier chapters the negotiation of the stay-alive contract was discussed. There are those occasions when the client refuses to enter into a stay-alive contract. When the client does refuse, and states, "I will kill myself before 'X' time, by 'Y' method no matter what you, or anybody else does," this constitutes the ultimate suicidal risk. At this point the counselor has no other choice but to consider hospitalization. There are many types of hospitalizations varying as to the type of hospital, types of treatment approaches available, and the type of patient the hospital will accept.

The optimal approach to hospitalization is to have the client come to accept your recommendation to be hospitalized, and voluntarily agree to admit himself to the hospital for evaluation and treatment. Very often this can be broached with the client by stating "Since you are not willing to state you will not kill yourself, my concern is that you will. I am obligated to do everything in my power to keep you alive. At this time I cannot trust your judgment and therefore I must trust mine in exercising what is in your best interest. I must make all attempts to see that your safety is assured. The only controlled environment that will provide the kind of protection you desperately need, at this time, would be a hospital. I am, therefore, going to make the necessary arrangements for you to admit yourself to the hospital."

This recommended type of dialogue stresses a number of important points. First, it emphasizes the counselor's willingness to take control. Very often, clients on the surface would appear to resist this. In reality, they are usually relieved that at last someone is going to take care of them. That is why it is important for the counselor to make all of the hospitalization arrangements. Also by structuring it in this manner, if the client is going to refuse to go along with your recommendation, it requires him to assert himself. Very often the client does not have the psychic energy for such assertion, and consequently the client is willing to go along with the counselor's recommendation and often does so by making comments such as, "I don't care what you do."

Secondly, this type of recommendation for hospitalization allows the client to feel that he is not going to be "locked away," since it is a voluntary hospitalization and the client may leave the hospital any time he so desires. It is important to stress this to the client, and it is an excellent "selling" point in trying to get the client to accept your recommendation.

The important issue here is that when the client becomes suicidal to the point that a threat is imminent, the counselor does not have the choice as to whether to hospitalize or not; the counselor must hospitalize. If the counselor did not hospitalize knowing the above risk, and the client had a serious or successful attempt, the counselor could be held responsible and would have to deal with the allegation of negligence. Therefore, the counselor is attempting to hospitalize the client for the client's protection as well as taking those actions that would protect the counselor from potential legal reprisals.

TYPES OF HOSPITALIZATIONS

Hospitalizations are of two types: voluntary and involuntary.

Voluntary hospitalization requires the client to "sign himself in" to a community or state hospital. Two things are required prior to this being done. First, it is necessary to find a physician, preferably a psychiatrist, who is on the staff of the hospital being considered and is willing to admit the client. Second, the client must demonstrate the ability to pay for the services that will be provided for him during his hospital stay. Most often, the client only has to present his health insurance identification card number. Hopefully the coverage of the client's health plan will be adequate to pay for the vast majority of his hospital expenses, but the client must demonstrate the ability to pay for those expenses not covered in his insurance plan prior to his admission to the hospital. Therefore, it is important for the counselor to find out as much information about the client's ability to pay for his hospitalization before the client is subjected to these inquiries by someone in the hospital's admitting office. All of this is done in order to prevent difficulties in admission for the client upon his arrival at the hospital. If the client encounters too many admission difficulties, it could precipitate the client's reconsideration of his decision to admit himself to the hospital.

Counselors are often under the mistaken belief that in order to hospitalize a client all they have to do is have the patient taken to a hospital. When this is done, the patient will, in all likelihood, be evaluated by the emergency room physician, who is unlikely to be a psychiatrist. Further, it is quite probable that the emergency room physician does not have admitting privileges. In this event it then becomes necessary for the emergency room physician to seek out a physician, hopefully a psychiatrist, who would be willing to admit the client under his service in the hospital. This may cause undue delay in the hospitalization of the client, and perhaps even result in the patient being denied admission to the hospital if the emergency room physician cannot find a psychiatrist that is willing to admit the client. At this point the client may become resistant and leave.

Another point to consider in voluntary admission is that many hospitals, particularly community hospitals, will not admit actively suicidal patients. There are a number of reasons for this kind of hospital policy. Many smaller hospitals do not have a psychiatric ward; therefore, the psychiatric patient must be admitted to a medical/surgical unit. This is an unfortunate situation for both the suicidal client as well as the other patients on the unit. The suicidal client is upsetting to the other patients, and for the suicidal patient there is often the embarrassment of being in the hospital for emotional reasons.

Another reason many hospitals will not admit the suicidal client is the hospital does not have the necessary setting or staffing to provide the necessary security precautions to treat the suicidal individual.

All of these potential problems, however, can be avoided if the counselor makes the necessary inquiries and arrangements for the client prior to the client's arrival at the hospital. It cannot be stressed enough how important these prehospitalization arrangements are. If these arrangements are not made in every detail, there is the extreme risk that the client will be lost in the communication cracks, and further will be unwilling to again subject himself to another attempt at hospitalization, thereby further exacerbating an already acute suicidal risk.

Another point to consider in the voluntary hospitalization is for the counselor to have direct contact with the psychiatrist prior to the patient's arrival at the hospital. The psychiatrist should be informed of the counselor's diagnostic impression; the client's previous history, particularly of previous hospitalizations for suicide attempts; and an assessment of the client's present suicidal risk. Once the psychiatrist has this information he is in the position to call the hospital with admitting orders. Hopefully, this direct contact with the psychiatrist will also allow the psychiatrist to be available to the client once the client arrives at the hospital.

Of course, the best possible situation is the one in which the counselor has established a working relationship with a physician, preferably a psychiatrist, prior to the onset of a crisis. This would ensure a working relationship between the counselor and the psychiatrist. The psychiatrist would then, hopefully, be in the position of having developed confidence in the counselor's diagnostic abilities, particularly with respect to suicidal risk. He would, therefore, more likely act upon the input of the counselor in the crisis situation. It is strongly urged that a counselor develop such a working relationship with a member of the medical community.

Involuntary hospitalization, sometimes referred to as "commitment," becomes necessary when the client is acutely suicidal and is unwilling to voluntarily admit himself to a hospital. Involuntary hospitalization is a legal act in which a magistrate or judge remands the patient to the custody of the hospital, most often a state medical facility. In effect, the patient is incarcerated against his will. In most states, current commitment criteria make it necessary for the counselor to demonstrate that the client represents a clear and imminent danger to himself or others.

Traditional psychodiagnostic categories, in and of themselves, do not constitute grounds for commitment. In most states commitment criteria were developed in order to protect the civil rights of their populace. Therefore, psychosis is no longer considered justification for legally mandated hospitalization in states which use the "imminent danger" criteria. Behavioral criteria for the imminence of danger must be demonstrated in order for the client to be committed. The rigor of the behavioral criteria varies widely from state to state and is interpreted differently among judges. In some states, it may be required that the counselor actually witness a suicidal attempt or gesture; in other states, it is only necessary for the client to verbally threaten suicide in the counselor's presence.

Who may initiate a commitment procedure varies widely from state to state. In many states a licensed physician is required. Further a psychiatrist may be required to evaluate the patient prior to admission. There is also variability as to how many physicians and/or psychiatrists may be necessary to initiate commitment procedures. Most states only require the written opinion of one physician, while others may require two. It is also possible, in some states, for the counselor himself to initiate the commitment procedure. In this instance, the counselor is in effect swearing out a complaint to a peace officer in order for the client to be picked up, brought to a hospital, and then evaluated by a psychiatrist. The psychiatrist then gives his opinion in writing to a judge or magistrate, who in turn makes the ultimate decision as to whether to remand the client to the custody of the hospital. In all these procedures, it is the judge who makes the final determination to commit or not to commit.

In those states requiring a physician to initiate the procedure, the counselor will still have to be actively involved in the hospitalization process. It would be the counselor's responsibility to initially contact the physician who would make the evaluation. Very often the patient's family physician can be used in this situation, particularly if the family physician knows the patient fairly well. If the client is not presently under a physician's care, there may be a problem for the counselor in finding a physician willing to evaluate the patient, since most physicians are quite reluctant to get involved with a potential commitment procedure for fear of liability issues. In this situation, the counselor may have a working relationship with a physician through his work setting, such as a consulting psychiatrist, a school or college physician.

Once a physician is contacted, the counselor has a difficult task in front of him; to somehow convey the seriousness of the situation and seek his support in the hospitalization process. This is particularly difficult if it is the first time the counselor has dealt with the physician. The key in illiciting the physician's support is to give the factual information as the counselor knows it including diagnostic impression, previous suicidal history, and the present threatening behaviors.

In any case, when it is a physician who must initiate the commitment procedure, he must to a large extent rely on the information provided by the counselor. It is important, then, that the counselor be physically present when the physician is filling out the commitment forms in order to provide him with the necessary information.

In the situation in which the counselor may initiate the commitment procedure it is usually required that he contact a local law enforcement official, most often a member of the county sheriff's office. The officer of the sheriff's office should be given the information previously mentioned. The officer should then be requested to bring the commitment request forms to your office. When the officer has arrived, he will assist you in filling out the form. When this has been completed, he will bring the form (which is actually a citizen's complaint) to the county magistrate. The county magistrate will in turn issue an order for the client to be taken into custody by the sheriff's office contingent upon the magistrate's agreement with your assessment of the imminent suicidal risk.

Once the judge has issued the order, the sheriff, or his designee, will attempt to locate the client, and having done so, will use whatever means necessary to transport the client to the nearest facility which will accept patients who have been committed for any emergency diagnostic detention. Most often this will be a state hospital, in that most private and community hospitals will not accept these patients.

It is in the counselor's best interest that he request of the police officer that when the client has been picked up the officer notify the counselor. This will allow the counselor to begin the next critical step, contact with the admitting physician on duty at the hospital to which the patient is being transported. The reason this step is so important is that it allows the counselor to have direct contact with the physician who will be making the determination as to what to do with the client. The counselor's input is particularly important in that many clients, either during transport or upon arrival at the hospital, "regroup" and may appear quite normal during the admitting evaluation. The client will often deny any suicidal intent in order to avoid hospitalization. If the admitting physician is forewarned of the client's condition and has the opportunity to have many of his questions answered before seeing the client, he is in a better position not to be taken in by the client's "flight into health." Another recommendation to consider is for the counselor to request the admitting physician contact the counselor after the evaluation of the patient is completed in order that the counselor may know the final decision regarding the client's hospitalization.

If the above steps do not occur, the counselor runs the risk of the client being denied admission to the hospital because of the lack in continuity of information flow. Further, once the client has suffered this embarrassment, it is extremely unlikely he would return to the counselor. He has also been taught not to talk about suicide. Therefore, he may be lost to the mental health care delivery system while still being actively suicidal. It is important for the counselor to realize once he has initiated the commitment procedure he has made the implicit decision to protect the life of his client, while in all probability sacrificing his therapeutic relationship with the client. The client will feel his confidential relationship had been violated. The client would be reluctant, ever again, to trust that communication in the counseling relationship would be held in confidence and consequently would never seek out help from a mental health professional. This is why it is critical that nothing go wrong in the commitment process.

In light of the extreme variability from state to state and, in some instances, from county to county in commitment procedures, it is strongly recommended that the counselor thoroughly familiarize himself with the commitment laws and procedures of his state and county before a suicidal crisis occurs. This information may be obtained through the counselor's local, county, or state law enforcement officials.

WHAT TO REALISTICALLY EXPECT
FROM HOSPITALIZATION

Counselors, as is true of the general public, often have naive assumptions concerning the type and amount of care a patient will receive while hospitalized for an emotional disability. This confusion is further compounded in that there is a wide range of treatment likely to be offered depending on the particular type of hospital to which the client is admitted.

If the client voluntarily admits himself to a community hospital with a relatively small psychiatric unit, the patient is very likely to receive daily contact with his psychiatrist, as well as frequent contact with nursing personnel. The patient will, in all probability, not be in the hospital for more than two weeks. Community-based care also has the advantage of not removing the client from his support system. It also has the advantage of the client avoiding the stigma of having been sent to a "mental hospital." Unfortunately, there are too few community hospitals that have the facilities to treat the suicidal patient.

If the client is committed to a state hospital, the counselor can expect his client will receive a very different type of care. The authors recently found it necessary to have a client committed to just such a facility. The client was committed on a Tuesday afternoon. On the following Monday the client contacted her counselor who had initiated the commitment procedure. During the intervening time, the client reported having been seen by her psychiatrist for one-half hour, and her social worker for an hour. When the counselor spoke with the psychiatrist and the social worker, neither of them spoke English as their native language and understanding them was very difficult. This example is all too common in state hospitals due to decreased funding, staffing shortages, as well as a limited number of qualified psychiatrists who are willing to work in the state hospital setting.

There is a great deal of variation with respect to the amount of time a patient will be involuntarily hospitalized. Commitments range anywhere from seven to ninety days. The length of hospital stay for a committed patient may be a function of the length of stay specified in the commitment order rather than of the patient's progress during the hospitalization.

MEDICATION AND SHOCK THERAPIES

Assuming the patient is significantly depressed upon hospitalization, treatment will very likely include the use of the tricyclic antidepressants. The tricyclics are medications which act by changing the biochemical causes of some depressions, namely the balance of certain chemicals in the brain which have been shown to be related to depression. These medications take from ten days to three weeks before the antidepressant effects become evident.

If the patient is agitated as well as depressed, the patient will probably be administered a major tranquilizing drug such as Thorazine® or Haldol®. These tranquilizers are used in order to bring the patient "under control." Once these major tranquilizers are indicated, the patient will probably be on them for at least one week, or until the agitation is no longer present.

On occasion, the major tranquilizers will be used in combination with the tricyclic antidepressants. The benefit of using the major tranquilizers concurrently with the antidepressants is that it allows the patient to be calmed by the tranquilizers while waiting for the antidepressants to take effect.

If, however, the client is "hell bent" on suicide and the risk is acutely imminent, the hospital staff may not have the luxury of time in waiting for the effects of medication. At the core of this is the fear that the client will kill himself and will fight the effects of the medications. In this situation, the only recourse is the initiation of electroconvulsive shock therapy. The concept of shock therapy is both a foreign and unpleasant one to most counselors. Gone are the days when shock was widely employed. But we as counselors must accept the fact that although the reasons for shock therapy's effectiveness is not understood, it is effective. Appleton (1976) in a review of the literature comparing the effectiveness of shock therapy with the antidepressants found ECT to be more effective in most studies.

It is important to point out that shock therapy is the exception and not the rule. Most often the patient can be controlled with the major tranquilizers, and further most depressions will respond to the antidepressants. Those depressions that will most favorably respond to the antidepressants are those that have a heavy endogenous loading (see endogenous depression, Chapter 2). The usual course of treatment trial with the tricyclic antidepressants is four weeks. If the patient has not improved in that time, it is unlikely the tricyclics will be effective. If the treatment trial of the tricyclics is unsuccessful, the psychiatrist has one of two options available. He may try a course of treatment using a monoamine oxidase inhibitors (MAOI) which is another class of major antidepressant medications.

This treatment would also take three to four weeks before any antidepressant effects would be observed. These medications are usually not initially used in preference to the tricyclics, since their side effects are usually more dangerous.

More likely, however, the psychiatrist would choose to use ECT in the event of the tricyclic failure. This choice is the more probable since, if the patient is still suicidal, the physician cannot afford to allow any more time to elapse in finding an effective treatment for the depression. The ECT is more likely to produce antidepressant effects than the MAOI and do so more quickly.

In the event the antidepressants were effective, one can expect the client to remain on the antidepressants for at least three months. Improvements with the antidepressants are gradual. First signs of improvement are more likely to be in vegetative signs, such as the improvement of appetite, improvement in sleeping, weight gain, increasing interest in the environment. It is unlikely at this time that the patient will report feeling any better; however, as mentioned earlier in Chapter 2, this can be a very dangerous time for the patient. His energy has increased, and yet the patient does not report feeling any better. The suicidal risk once again "rears its ugly head." However, after about four weeks the crisis will subside because the client will report feeling less depressed and consequently less, or not, suicidal.

WHAT TO EXPECT FROM PSYCHIATRISTS

In our culture, when all else fails in suicide intervention, we put people in hospitals. Often the motivation for hospitalization is multiple on the part of the counselor. Of course, one motivation is to get the client to a "safe place" in that the counselor has concluded that it is no longer possible to exert suicidal precautions in the client's environment. Another motivation, that is less often explicit, is the counselor's need to get the client "off his hands" for fear the client will kill himself while under the care of the counselor. Finally, a last motivation is for the counselor "to cover himself" and get the client to the treatment facility our society prescribes for those who are actively suicidal. If the counselor does not hospitalize a client who according to evidence is actively suicidal, and if he does kill himself, the counselor could be held negligent. Since our society designates hospitalization as the reasonable course of action, and since the patient is under the care of a psychiatrist, it makes the psychiatrist the "ultimate authority" on suicide.

Is such faith in the expertise of a psychiatrist with respect to suicide justified? Light (1973) states that residency programs in psychiatry are not likely to provide systematic instruction in suicidal care. He further contends the training a psychiatrist receives in suicide intervention is no better or no worse than professional training in suicidal intervention in any of the other mental health disciplines. Most training programs in the mental health disciplines of counseling, psychology, or social work do not even include a course in their curriculum in suicide.

Nevertheless, the "buck stops" with the psychiatrist. It is small wonder then that the psychiatrist relies so heavily on the one aspect of mental health care that sets him apart from the other mental health specialties — medication.

It is further important to point out that the psychiatrist is probably seeing someone else's client who has become so actively suicidal that hospitalization became necessary. Further, once the suicidal crisis has passed and the patient is discharged from the hospital, it is unlikely that the patient will remain in the care of the psychiatrist. The patient will probably return to the counselor who was the initial therapist.

In summation, we refer people whom we feel no longer able to treat to a psychiatrist whose training and expertise in suicide prevention is probably no better than the counselor's. We implicitly say to the psychiatrist "Save this person's life." Once the client is "saved" and is now "safe" for the counselor, we request the psychiatrist return the client to our care. This is particularly true for the patient who has been committed. The committed patient is unlikely to see the psychiatrist more than once a week. The committed patient will probably be in group therapy for one to two hours per week, and the group therapy will likely be led by a social worker, not a psychiatrist. The care this patient receives could hardly be called intensive psychiatric care, and yet that is often what the naive counselor assumes his client receives.

What then is the major treatment effect?

One cannot dismiss the importance of chemotherapy in allowing the patient to gain control. Perhaps a more significant effect upon the suicidal client in the state hospital is the "shock effect" of being there. Most suicidal patients are not psychotic, but they are placed in the environment that is charged with the care of psychotics. This is often quite disconcerting to the suicidal client. The suicidal client comes to realize that if he does not "get better" his fate is the confines of the hospital. On many occasions one can hear the suicidal client describe his feelings of being with people who were "really crazy" and therefore he would do anything to get out of the hospital. Sometimes the client may attempt a flight into health in order to be dismissed. Perhaps as often, the hospital setting provides a reality testing for the client by which he can come to evaluate the "relative" severity of his problem when compared to the other hospital patients. The result of this comparison often leads the client to place his problems in a less serious perspective.

Another positive effect of hospitalization is that it allows the patient to be removed from the life stress situations that precipitated the crisis. The patient has the opportunity to rest and have others take care of him. This allows the client to reevaluate his life situation more objectively, in that the stressors are not as close to him.

There is some danger, however, in assuming that once the patient is well enough to be discharged from the hospital he is no longer suicidal. The counselor must keep in mind that people who kill themselves are more likely to do so within a month after discharge from the hospital than when in the hospital. In summation, hospitalization is at best a stop gap measure to keep the client alive during the hospital stay and should not be viewed as the ultimate answer to suicide prevention.

REFERENCES

Appleton, William S.: Third psychoactive drug usage guide. *Dis Nerv Syst,* *37(1)*:39-51, 1976.

Light, Donald W., Jr.: Treating suicide: the illusions of a professional movement. *Am Soc Service J, 25*:475-487, 1973.

AUTHOR INDEX

A

Ackerman, J. Mark, 64, 80, 81
Allen, George N., 14
Anderson, Dorothy B., 40
Anderson, Scott, 98, 99, 100
Appleton, William S., 110, 114

B

Barnes, Graham, 63
Basescu, Sabert, 83, 85
Bassuk, Ellen L., 19, 22, 29
Beck, Aaron T., 27, 29, 40
Bellak, Leopold, 64
Bergum, Thomas, 98, 99, 100
Bersoff, Donald N., 95, 100
Boswell, John W., 38, 39
Brockopp, Gene W., 93
Brown, Michael, 64

C

Cain, Albert C., 81
Collins, William, ix

D

Delworth, Ursula, 93
Dorpat, Theodore L., 38, 39
Durkheim, Emile, 14

E

Ellis, Edward R., 14

F

Farber, Maurice L., 36, 39
Farberow, Norman L., 14, 16, 27, 29, 39
Fisher, Sheila A., 64, 93

Fox, Renee C., 95, 100
Frederick, Calvin J., 4, 8, 14, 34, 39, 64

G

Ganzler, Sidney, 36, 39
Gibbs, Jack P., 14
Goulding, Mary, ix
Goulding, Robert, ix
Grollman, Earl A., 64

H

Hamilton, Donald M., 64
Helgason, Tomas, 18, 29
Hendrie, Hugh C., 18, 29
Hillman, James, 14
Huige, Kristyn, 64

K

Kiev, Ari, 40
Klagsbrun, Francine, 14
Kobler, Arthur L., 14
Krauss, Herbert H., 14

L

Lamb, Charles W., 93
Larsson, Tage, 14
Leonard, Calista V., 64
Lester, David, 11, 14, 27, 29, 35, 38, 39, 93
Lester, Gene, 14
Lettieri, Dan J., 35, 39, 40
Levy, Charles S., 94, 100
Light, Donald W., 82, 85, 112, 114
Litman, Robert E., 14, 16, 27, 29, 83, 85
Ljungstedt, Nils, 14

M

Maluccio, Anthony N., 65, 73

115

Maris, Ronald W., 6, 14
Marlow, Wilma D., 65, 73
McClean, Lenora J., 40
McEvoy, Theodore, 35, 39
Meerloo, Joost A. M., 4, 14
Mendel, Werner M., 64
Miles, Charles P., 18, 27, 29
Moss, Leonard M., 64

N

Neuringer, Charles, 12, 14, 32, 39
Nothmann, Gerhard, ix

O

Orten, James D., 93

P

Paykel, Eugene S., 18, 29
Peck, Michael L., 28, 29
Pokorney, Alex D., 18, 28, 29
Pretzell, Paul W., 60, 63

R

Resnik, H. L. P., 14, 40, 64
Rudrow, Edward H., 93

S

Schoonover, Stephen C., 19, 22, 29
Shelton, John L., 64, 80, 81
Shneidman, Edwin S., 12, 14, 16, 27, 29
Shorr, Joseph E., 64
Sifneos, Peter E., 93
Sinnett, E. Robert, 64, 93
Small, Leonard, 64
Spiro, Saul, ix
Stone, Alan A., 64
Stotland, Ezra, 14

T

Taub, Janet, 93
Taylor, Eugene, ix
Thompson, George, ix
Thompson, Kay C., 18, 29
Tsuang, Ming, 28, 29
Tuckman, Jacob, 89, 93

W

Waldenstrom, Jan, 14
Winokur, George, 28, 29
Wolman, Benjamin B., 14
Wolpe, Joseph, 64
Woollams, Stanley, 64
Worden, J. William, 35, 39

SUBJECT INDEX

A

Action plans, 44-45
Active listening, 41, 42, 87
Alcoholism, 28
Ambivalence, 46-47
Anger, suicide as an expression of, 48
Anhedonia, 27
Anorexia, 27

B

Biogenic amine hypothesis, 22
Bipolar psychotic depression, 20-21

C

Client variables, 46-59
Code of ethics, 95-97
  American Personnel and Guidance Association, 97, 100
  American Psychological Association, 95, 100
  Group for the Advancement of Psychiatry, Committee of Psychiatry and Law, 97, 100
Commitment (see Hospitalization, involuntary)
Confidentiality, 79, 94-97
Consultation with colleagues, 83-84, 99
Contact, early establishment of, 41-42
Continuity of treatment, 62-63, 75-76
Contract negotiation, diagnostic elements in, 71
Contracts
  against physical harm, 69-70
  broken, 70
  characteristics of, 65-66
Counseling process, variables in, 61-63
Counseling strategies, 41-63
Counselor as primary source of support,
74-76
Counselor variables, 59-61
Cry for help, 39

D

Depression
  in assessment of suicidal risk, 36
  types of, 15-27
    agitated, 16-17, 50-51
    endogenous, 22-24
    exogenous, 22-24, 110
    neurotic, 17-21
    primary, 24-27
    psychotic, bipolar, 20-21
    psychotic, unipolar, 18-20
    reactive, 22, 27
    retarded, 51-52
    secondary, 24-27
Directive therapy, need for, 60

E

Electroconvulsive shock therapy (ECT), 110, 111
Emergency room procedures, 71, 75
Emotion, ventilation of, 53-54
Ethical considerations (see Confidentiality)

F

Family, role of (see Significant others)
Family therapy, 77
Feedback, 55
Free will, 8, 13
Friends, role of (see Significant others)

G

Group counseling, 45, 66

117

Guilt, 27, 48, 56

H

Haplessness, 34
Helplessness, 34-35, 48-49
Hope, 43-44
Hopelessness, 27, 34, 48-49, 56
Hospitalization, 101-113
  counselor's role in, 19-20
  involuntary, 105-108
  realistic expectations, 108-109
  voluntary, 103-105
Humor, role of, in assessment of suicidal
  risk, 36

I

Impulse control, 52-53, 80
Inappropriate reaction of counselor, 61
Information gathering, 62
  via telephone, 87-90
Insomnia, 22, 35-36

L

Legal implications, 98-99
Lethality, assessment of, 32
Life line, 74-81
Life support activities, 79-81
Loss
  experience of, 22
  recent, 36

M

Malpractice, 98
Manic behavior, 21
Medication, 23, 109-111, 112
Mind racing, 54-55
Monoamine oxidase inhibitors (MAOI),
  110-111
Motive, 47-50

N

Negativism, 55-56
No-kill contract (*see* Stay-alive contract)

O

Organic brain syndrome, 28
Overgeneralization, 55
Over-reaction of counselor, 60

P

Patience, need for, 59
Permission, 44, 57, 58-59, 63
Personality disorders, 28
Physical energy, ventilation of, 53-54
Potency, 44, 57, 58-59, 63
Privileged communication, 94
Protection, 44, 63
Psychiatrists, realistic expectations of,
  111-113
Psychological autopsy, 7, 85
Psychomotor retardation, 27
"Putting the house in order," 36

R

Reaction to suicide, counselor's, 82-85
Redecisions, 59
Research, problems and limitations, 10-11
Rescue, likelihood of, 33
Responsibility, 56-57, 80
Role of family members (*see* Significant
  others)

S

Saving face, client's need for, 57-58
Scheduling, 61-62
Schizophrenia, suicidal risk in, 28-29, 38,
  52
Self-destructive personality, diagnosis of,
  30-39
Significant others, 23, 46, 51, 60, 76-79,
  82, 89, 95-96
  role of family, 23, 46, 51, 60, 76-79, 89, 96
  role of friends, 51, 60, 76, 78-79, 89
Stay-alive contract, 61, 63, 66-69, 94, 101
  refusal to agree to, 70-71
Suicidal crisis, duration of, 19, 37-38
Suicidal gesture, determinants of, 38-39
Suicidal risk, 23-24, 27, 28, 31-39, 101
Suicidal thoughts, 4, 9, 30-37

Suicide
 altruistic, 9
 anomic, 9
 classifications of, 11-13
 communication, as a means of, 50
 definition of, 3-4
 egoistic, 9
 family history related to, 35
 fatalistic, 9
 legal views of, 8
 psychological views of, 8-10
  Adler, 9
  Freud, 9
  Horney, 9
  Menninger, 9
  Sullivan, 9
 religious and philosophical views of, 7-8
  Camus, 7
  Hume, 7
 signs of, 27
 sociological views of, 8-10
  Durkheim, 9
  social theorists, 9
 statistics of, 4-7
  age groups, 5
  geographical areas, 5
  marital status, 6
  race, 6
  religion, 6
  season, 6
  sex, 5-6
  socioeconomic status, 6

T

Tarasoff v. Regents of University of California, 96
Telephone, use of, 86-92
 with regular client, 90-91
 with stranger in crisis, 86-89, 91-92
Termination of clients, 52
Thought stopping, 54
Tranquilizers, 110
Tricyclics, 23, 109-110
Trust, in counselor-client relationship, 60

U

Under-reaction of counselor, 60-61
Understanding, counselor expressions of, 42-43
Unipolar psychotic depression, 18-20